When My Faith Feels Shallow is a sharing of wisdom from a gracious lady who lived what she learned and learned what she lived. It is a book of healing, of helps, and of hope. It is a recipe book for the hungry, a valid dictionary for the one at a loss for words, and a readable map assuring the traveler of the best way home. In this book I find truth that is new and a reclaiming of old truths with fresh effectiveness. To the author I say, Thanks, I needed that!

—Jeannette Clift George,
author of John, His Story,
and star of the movie The Hiding Place

*F*aith depends on the depth of our belief. It is human nature to allow deep faith to become shallow. Minette Drumwright Pratt has developed a game plan that, if followed, can lead to victory in your life. All victories are rooted in basic fundamentals. Each of the pathways of *When My Faith Feels Shallow* is spiritually enlightening and allows the reader to seriously take on the mind of Christ. We recommend this book with the belief it can change your life and deepen your faith.

—Grant Teaff,
executive director of the American Football Coaches Association,
and
Donell Teaff,
member of the Baylor University Board of Regents and permanent
board member of the American Football Coaches' Wives Association

When Minette Drumwright Pratt states her intention to reveal her uncomplicated understandings of God's profound and trustworthy Word, her friends and readers know to expect the personal and challenging testimony of a lifelong seeker. Following her pathways toward a mature faith offers us a basic but profound direction toward a mature and meaningful life. *When My Faith Feels Shallow* is a must-read for the Christian man or woman who seeks deeper intimacy with God.

—Dr. Bill O'Brien,
founding director of The Global Center at Samford University
and missions professor at Beeson Divinity School, and
Dr. Dellanna O'Brien,
former Executive Director of Woman's Missionary Union

Written from her lifelong learning lab, Minette's words flow out of her pursuit of Kingdom living. Having walked with Minette as a missions advocate, a neighbor, her pastor's wife, a Habitat for Humanity wheelbarrow sidekick, and one of her adopted daughters, I've seen this book's message in her living. Now on the far side of the sea, the eternal truths Minette lived and poured into my life resound regularly in my faith walking. I love and know the Father better because of the image of Christ I've seen in Minette.

—Cindy Gaskins,
former Youth Consultant with Texas WMU
and pastor's wife for 20 years, with the last five spent at
International Baptist Church of Hong Kong

WHEN MY FAITH FEELS SHALLOW

Pursuing the Depths of God

MINETTE DRUMWRIGHT PRATT

new
hope
PUBLISHERS

Birmingham, Alabama

New Hope® Publishers
P. O. Box 12065
Birmingham, AL 35202-2065
www.newhopepublishers.com

Library of Congress Cataloging-in-Publication Data
Pratt, Minette Drumwright.
When my faith feels shallow : pursuing the depths of God / by Minette Drumwright Pratt.
p. cm.
ISBN 1-56309-773-7 (pbk.)
1.   Christian life. I. Title.
BV4501.3.P73 2004
248.4—dc22
2004005127

ISBN: 1-56309-773-7

N044116 • 0604 • 5M1

Dedication

If you know me, you are not surprised that I am dedicating this book to my new husband, Dr. William M. Pratt, Jr. Bill has patiently gone over every word of this manuscript with me. I read it aloud from my computer screen as he followed the contents on the hard copy. Having written a number of papers related to his graduate degrees, he is adept at grammar, sentence construction, form, and spotting my careless mistakes.

Since the actual writing of this book took place as our courtship unfolded, Bill could have easily considered this project as competition, or an impediment! Well, it *was*, really, but he never once complained. In fact, he was probably willing to complete it himself! You see, I had told him there would be no wedding until the manuscript got turned in. Now we have married, and even as I give my attention to the writing of this dedication, I hear him in our kitchen preparing our evening meal. Eat your hearts out, girls!

Thus, it is with my sweetest love and deepest joy that I dedicate this book to my Bill.

Table of Contents

Preface

I am so aware of the many helpful books related to the topic of this book that are lining the shelves of thousands of stores. The deeper I moved into this writing project, the more I questioned my ability to contribute to all that is already available.

The one matter that at least partially validates my attempt to write on this subject is that I am very knowledgeable personally about what it means to be shallow. I am aware of the ease that is involved in doing the "good, fine things" of the church, but *not* for the purpose of pursuing the depths and glory of God or moving toward Christlikeness. Of course, I believed in being sincere. I was not consciously trying to impress anyone with my "religiosity," although that may have hidden itself somewhere in the mix. Thinking back, I was probably vaguely conscious of a certain comfortable satisfaction in my "doing right" (at least, "sorta" right). Later, in my young adulthood, I would make the soul-shaking discovery that there was not much going on "beneath the waterline" of my life—within my own soul. I was just plain shallow!

I still struggle with experiences that remind me of my areas of shallowness. Perhaps we all do. In fact, I had another title for this book. However, after becoming aware of my story in the first draft of the manuscript, my editor and the title team guided me to reflect on my own confession of shallowness in the title of the book. They are convinced that *shallowness* is a familiar struggle to many (perhaps all)—even earnest followers of Christ.

In all fairness, let me warn you. If you expect this book to be a theological treatise, please drop it like a hot potato! At the same time, I want you to know of my deep commitment to simply follow and live the Word of God. With all my heart, I want to offer the Scriptures in a way that reveals their down-to-earth, common-sense, applicable guidance for our everyday lives. My deep desire and goal is that we will know our Lord better, love Him increasingly, and become more like Jesus as we make our way through these pages together.

Writing this book has happened at a most unusual time in my life. I did not plan it this way, of course. In fact, it was very inconvenient (!) to have a full-fledged, unexpected, unlooked-for, irresistible romance in the midst of this writing commitment, not to mention an already full calendar of involvements. You will not find this as a part of my story in the Introduction because I had actually written that part before my "surprise." I do want to share with you *now*—"up front," before you get into the manuscript—the latest twists and turns of my journey.

In a nutshell: In the summer of 2002, just as I agreed to the writing of this book, I received a letter from a long-time but casual friend, Dr. William Pratt. His deceased wife had been my good friend at Baylor. In fact, she and I had worked together one hot Texas summer on a team of college students doing Vacation Bible School work in small churches. These were situations where there would have been no VBS if energetic college kids had not descended upon the congregation and provided the impetus and leadership.

At the time I received *the letter* from Bill, I had been widowed for 21 years. I write rather fully about the profound segment of my life with my late husband, Dr. Huber Drumwright, in the Introduction. For now, suffice it to say that my testimony concerning those two decades as a widow is simple, but to me, profound. Again and again through the years, the words of our Lord as quoted by Isaiah kept looming before me: "I am going to do a new thing. See, I have already begun." Indeed, the Lord has been totally faithful every new step of the way, and given me many new opportunities of service that, even now, are beyond my comprehension.

Which takes me back to *the letter*. From that beginning touch point of *the letter*, I felt sparks in my heart. I will spare you the many delicious details until another time (except to say that Bill was writing me after reading my book *The Life That Prays*). Gradually (Bill would place emphasis on my "gradualness"), I fell in love with the writer of *the letter*. Only the Lord—and Bill—could have stirred (and melted) my rusty heart. After all these years of busy aloneness, no one could have been more surprised than I was, and am, even now, about those sparks and that stirring!

Our love for one another steadily intensified, and in due time Bill and I began thinking and talking seriously about the future together. My world again was dramatically changing. I recalled a quotation that had lodged in my mind many years ago: "In every change, there is a death and a rebirth."

I have pondered that statement many times. I believe there is wisdom in it. However, if I were to put that thought into my own words, I would say, "Every change—every new thing God brings to us—calls for us to release the honored past, and then embrace the challenging future."

Yes, another tremendous change—an incredible "new thing"—began to take place with *the letter*, and led to our marriage in July 2003. I have ultimate gratitude for my past. I deeply honor it. But our recent wedding day was the first day of a new future. In a sense, I *released* my wonderful past. I will not forget it. I will always cherish it. At the same time, I embraced the new future God had for me. And I prayed that day, as I do every day, the prayer that Dag Hammarskjold worded: "For all that has been, thanks. For all that will be, yes!" And I praise the Father's holy and wonderful Name.

Will you join Bill and me in praying, "Father, for all that has been, thanks. For all that will be, yes!" This stance will indeed deepen our souls and assist in leading us into the depths of God—to Christlikeness.

Minette Drumwright Pratt

Acknowledgments

*I*t is very important to me to recognize those who have been so helpful in the process of this writing project. My earliest "readers" were Dr. Al Fasol, Dr. David Crutchley, my daughters Meme Perry and Debra Underwood, Cindy Gaskins, and Dr. Duane Brooks. I am indebted to each of them for many demonstrations of their love through many years. They gave generously of their time, their helpful thoughts, comments, suggestions, and encouragement. My most special "mention" goes to Dr. William Pratt, who served as my first "copy editor" as he and I were in the midst of a wonderful courtship, making plans for marriage, and readying the manuscript for turning in to my editor. After our marriage, I promoted Bill to my "in-house copy editor." In the midst of this most unusual time in my life, he, along with the others I mentioned, has saved my sanity.

My special appreciation also goes to Rebecca England, my esteemed editor. Her sweet, gentle acceptance of working with this somewhat distracted writer—me—could have tried her patience, but she never indicated the least hint of that possibility. In fact, Rebecca has been delightfully unflappable. She has blessed me again and again. Also, Lynn Waldrep, media specialist for New Hope, has been a wonderful colleague and partner in the endless details of the project. I value deeply the friendship of these two gifted young professionals.

I acknowledge also the many writers—too many to name—whose books the Lord has used to bless me and teach me through many years (and they continue to have that role). Most of the authors I have never met. I am reminded every time I prepare to speak or write, but especially as I work through my own personal storms—as well as my joys—that the Father has used *them* in my life in extraordinary ways through the books they have written through the years.

This brings me to acknowledge that my deepest gratitude is to our Lord—for loving me, saving me, sustaining me through thick and thin, teaching me day by day to base my life on His Greatest Commandment and His Great Commission. All over again, I rededicate myself to loving Him, glorifying Him with great joy, and serving Him and others in the name of Jesus as I seek to take every opportunity I have to share His great Good News with others, where I live, and to the ends of the earth.

Introduction

Since you're reading this book, you're interested in pursuing the depths of God. You've felt some need to delve below the surface of your life and know God in an authentic way. Prepare yourself, because God never refuses this sort of invitation. If you seek to know God, He will reveal Himself to you.

I am not writing about this subject as though I have an inside track on spiritual depth. Conversely, I am drawn to the topic because I myself *have* lived a Christian life that *appeared* spiritual, but was not authentic. Not that I was intentionally unreal—in fact, I did not have a clue that I was.

Even now, after many years of commitment to transparency and depth in my relationship with God and people, I still struggle with the issue, and I find myself falling short. However, for too long a time, I was oblivious to the lack of realness in myself.

Perhaps it is appropriate to share more specifically from my own story. I grew up in a pastor's home, surrounded by "involvement plus" in our church. My parents were well-meaning to the extreme. They loved the Lord, and they earnestly wanted their children to live lives dedicated to Him—and to be models for the congregation to use as the pattern for their own children. I could be wrong, of course, but it seemed to me that conforming to the "rules"—and to what my mother and father perceived to be the expectations of the congregation—was a major goal of their parenting. And they longed for their earnestness to be matched by all our congregation.

Daddy pastored the same church in San Antonio, Texas, for 25 years—a span that included all my growing-up years. I suppose our church was typical for that era: evangelistic, missions-minded, revivalistic (two revivals a year, two weeks in length), no card playing, no dancing, no movies, no exceptions! I had a sneaking suspicion that we preacher's kids were the only ones who were actually held to these stringent expectations.

My parents' precepts were reflected in the large number of rules we were expected to follow. In our home, there was superb communication about all the expectations. However, it has been "scientifically established" that in any preacher's family with three kids, at least one of them will have problems with the rules. In our family, I was that one! I just plain broke some of the rules, and put hairline fractures in many others.

Punishment was a peach tree switch. We had a beautiful peach tree in our back yard. At least, it started out that way. My parents killed our peach tree—on me! I even got a switching one day when I said, "Oh look, our switch tree has a peach on it." You see, one of our rules was, "Thou shalt not be a smart aleck." That was the rule that got me in the most trouble. I survived my childhood, but our peach tree did not.

Our lives revolved around our church activities. Mother made sure that the missions organizations were fully staffed and operating. Seeds were planted early that, later in my life, would grow and flourish. Our church sponsored a Mexican mission that met every Sunday afternoon. I have many memories of going with Mother and Daddy to round up the children and then "help" with their classes. In the brief service that followed the classes, Daddy always told a Bible story and shared "how to be saved." Over the years, many made professions of faith.

Also, my mother gave (free, of course) piano lessons to any and all who wanted to take them. She taught them not the usual "Minuet in G," but hymns. During the many years of her teaching, she prepared a number of the children to become church pianists for Hispanic congregations in our city.

My parents worked hard serving God and our congregation. They had high expectations not only of us kids, but of themselves as servants of the Lord. As a child, I was slightly embarrassed by their intense dedication. However, I grew to be very proud of them, to appreciate their sheer fineness, and to be grateful for my heritage.

My memory does not include any time when I was not aware of the love of God in Jesus. It was a part of the conversation and the atmosphere of our home. One Sunday evening when I was 9, Daddy and I were walking to church together. Mother, Dodie, and Glen were coming later in the car. As we walked hand-in-hand down Santa Monica Street, we got into a conversation about Jesus. This had happened a number of times, but on this evening, I understood in a new dimension that Jesus' love was for *me,* personally, and He died on the cross for *my* sins so I could live in heaven with Him forever. In a very simple way, I asked Jesus to forgive my sins and come live in my heart.

I understood very little of what I was asking. To borrow someone else's words, "All I understood of myself, I gave to all I understood of Jesus." It was very childlike, but it was real. I meant it. I treasure that beginning of my spiritual life.

My home and my church represent those who took patient—and at times impatient—interest in teaching me, affirming me, caring about me, rebuking me, discipling me, and nurturing me. They gave me many opportunities to learn the things of the Lord. My home and my church were imperfect, as they are for all of us, but I acknowledge gratefully the multiple attempts many earnest people made to show me the way. Looking back, however, I must also acknowledge that there was not much going on in my soul.

I do recall one exception. As a young teenager, I attended youth missions camp at Alto Frio, in the beautiful Texas hill country. During the invitation at the concluding service, I walked down the aisle under the old tabernacle and rededicated my life. To me, that meant I was willing to know God's plan for my life. It was another spiritual marker in my young life, and it truly "marked" my heart. Later I learned that, as significant as my decision was, the most important reality was to know God, and to know His heart. Somehow I had missed this understanding. Later, knowing Him would become my passion.

Back to my earlier years. I went off to college *not* intending to marry a preacher—in fact, intending *not* to marry a preacher. But I met one who was irresistible, and I married him—Huber Drumwright. We moved as bride and groom to a little farming village, Huber's student pastorate. Soon he was pastoring a new church in a booming part of north Dallas. At the same time, he began teaching as an instructor at Southwestern Seminary, which meant commuting from Dallas to Fort Worth. And he was working—haphazardly at that point—on his doctorate. We lived a hectic, harried, hurried life, juggling activities, events, and commitments in both cities.

There were times, as he kissed me "goodbye," when he would say, wrinkling his brow, "Honey, I have not had time to write the pastor's column for the church bulletin, and it is due today. Would you please write it for me?" I was barely 21 years old when I wrote my first pastor's column!

After four years of pastoring in Dallas, Huber resigned our church. We moved to Forth Worth to enable him to give focused attention to his deadline for completing his doctorate. He continued to teach a full load of seminary classes. A nearby country church called him as pastor, and he accepted. One big difference was that this little church did not even have a pastor's column! He soon finished his Th.D.

After six years of teaching at Southwestern Seminary, Huber was eligible for a sabbatical leave. He chose to pursue special study in his field of New Testament and Greek at Princeton Seminary in New Jersey. As an afterthought, I signed up for two courses. One of my choices was a class on prayer and worship. I did not expect to encounter anything new. After all, I had spent my life in the middle of prayer and worship. Yet the Lord used the class and the godly professor to cause me to make some disturbing discoveries about myself. The Holy Spirit brought to my attention the fact that while I was believing all the "right" things, and doing "good" things, I was shallow in my soul and shallow in my understanding of the real meaning of prayer and worship. This meant I was *shallow* in my relationship with God in Christ. I further realized how lacking I was in the power and spiritual energy God makes available through His Holy Spirit for the living of daily life.

Shallow and lacking—those two terribly descriptive words loomed up before me, and I knew they were accurate. The old phrase came to my mind: I was "a mile wide and an inch deep." This was hard to take, for here I was a pastor's daughter, a pastor's wife, a seminary professor's wife, and I was seeing myself as God saw me in the depths of my heart.

I was beyond humbled—I felt broken before Him. I tasted contriteness. . . .

Deep within, I heard the still, small voice of Jesus saying, lovingly, "Learn from Me. Open your life to what I want to teach you and do within you." I felt a stirring all through my being. I knew I wanted Jesus to be my teacher. With all my heart, I wanted to know Him intimately. It was then that a desire was born deep within me to become an authentic follower of Christ.

He began to teach me. I am sure I missed many of His lessons, but I relished the days I discerned a new truth from Him. I remember that period as providing a series of meaningful spiritual markers forever impacting my relationship with the Savior.

For example, I was invited by a group to teach a certain book—*A Practical Primer on Prayer.* I am not sure that book meant anything extraordinary to anyone who heard me teach that day, but the Lord used the book to make a difference in *my* life. To this day, I continue to submit to many of the spiritual disciplines the little book suggested.

Overall, God used the class I briefly described (for a fuller description, see my book *The Life That Prays*) and the book I taught to help me make discoveries of and commitments to some important disciplines sorely absent from my life. In short, in the midst of that combination of events, the Lord showed me my own shallowness. He showed me that prayer and all the matters of the soul must be an integral part of my *daily inner life*—real, heartfelt prayer—not just routine, prayer-type words, but authentic words and thoughts that come from staying closely connected to Christ day and night. I felt a new longing to know Him and His heart closely and intimately. It was then that my longing became a quiet passion.

The bottom line of my experience was that I discerned a clear, definite leading to be a serious pray-er, especially for God's mission in the world and those who do not know Him. Today we would say God was calling me to a ministry of prayer. I took His call seriously. And I believe at that point He gave me a heart for prayer. Soon I learned that God calls *every* believer to a ministry of prayer, and He gives to *everyone* who will receive it a heart for prayer.

It was then that Jesus' words in John 15 became so meaningful to me: "I am the Vine; you are the branch." I take it personally as He says to me daily, "Stay connected closely to Me. Only then will you receive the resources that flow from the vine into the life of the branches. Only as you do so will you bear fruit—your role in the Kingdom." He taught me this is the secret of life in Him—simply being a fruitful branch, receiving the flow of His resources consistently, every day, in every circumstance. In fact, I realized He had been speaking to me all along, but now I was hearing and responding.

At the end of the leave, our family returned to Fort Worth. Outwardly, I looked the same, but inwardly, my soul was being transformed. There was a new joy, a new energy, a quiet, deep fulfillment beyond anything I had experienced before. Jesus had indeed become my daily teacher.

As time unfolded, the Lord led me into a variety of ministries, some related to prayer and the inward journey of being close to Him. At the same time, He was clear about His expectation that I was to be a *doer* of His Word, not just a reader or a hearer. Christ led me into ministries having to do with my outward journey with Him—avenues of service through our church and our church's ministries, and some outside that framework. For example, I worked with unwed mothers. Every Thursday morning for 12 years, I taught a Bible class of economically disadvantaged women—and they taught me so much! I led a women's Bible study in the federal prison in Fort Worth. I also worked with internationals. Not all of this at once, of course, but over the years. I was simply responding to God's *daily* leadership. Frankly, I could not *not* do what I did.

I think my family sensed my joy. In our family prayertime each morning, in addition to praying for missionaries, we prayed for one another in specific, intentional ways. One morning, Debra, our younger daughter, was praying first, and she began praying for her sister. "Dear God, Meme is so worried about that awful test she has been studying for. Please help her to do her best and to remember all that stuff she studied…and bless Daddy, dear God, as he works in his office at the seminary, and be with Him as He teaches the students how to understand the Bible and how to preach and teach about Jesus…and dear God, be with Moms as she—" she paused with one of those pregnant pauses and it crossed my mind, "Ummmmmm, I am about to see how my child perceives my day, and all the things I do." She repeated herself— "Bless Moms," another pause—"as she plays around all day!"

They laughed out loud. I admit it—my sense of humor went south. I was thinking, "I have got to impress upon this kid that my days are *full* of worthwhile things. She does not understand. I am *not* out there just having fun all day."

Then it dawned on me. "Oh, yes, I am," I admitted to myself. "She's right. I am having so much joy—real joy, God-given joy—and she is catching accurately the essence of what I am feeling about my day-by-day journey with the Lord. I would not word it exactly the way she did. But in her childish discernment, she was tuning in to the joy I was experiencing.

In 1980, Huber experienced a powerful call from the Lord to serve as executive director of the Arkansas Baptist Convention. In due time, we made the move to Little Rock, expecting a major adjustment in the change. Although we missed our longtime friends and colleagues, we instantly felt we were indeed *home*. In my experience, that comes with being where God leads you.

With both of our daughters happily in college at Baylor, Huber and I spent every weekend and sometimes weekdays traveling the state and working with the churches. Huber called it "our running around together." It was an exhilarating time. But that joyful period lasted only 14 months.

In 1981, with no warning, Huber suffered a fatal heart attack. To put it mildly, I was traumatized and devastated. We had nearly 31 years together, and our many plans and dreams crashed and burned in an instant. Our girls and I had our individual and collective struggles with *how to do life* without him.

Several months into that wrenching time frame, I was contacted by the (then) Foreign Mission Board about joining their staff in Richmond. Gradually, I developed a sense of rightness and a sense of call about investing myself in what they were asking me to do. Still broken from my loss, I moved east instead of west, away from my roots and family ties. That move became another major spiritual marker in my life. I would never have chosen that chapter—living life apart from Huber—but God was faithful in the midst of life's most devastating loss.

I believed with all my heart in the work I was responsible for leading—calling individuals and churches to a life of prayer involvement with God and others and the world. One day it dawned on me. What I was doing was calling others to make the very same commitment I had made many years earlier in that little New Jersey town: to know God and His heart intimately and become meaningfully involved, through prayer, in what He was doing in the world. It was a new, yet

27

old, work I was doing. Isn't it amazing how God weaves together the threads of our lives into entirely new designs? In the midst of painful circumstances, God had given me a wonderful gift of ministry.

I went to Richmond thinking I would be there several years and then return to Texas. However, I got so caught up in the work I was doing that by the time I returned to Texas I had been away sixteen years. Every day was—and is—a joy and a gift. By the way, I am still just playing around all day!

Have you given yourself to the priority of knowing the Father, and His heart and will and Word and voice? Has He given you a heart for prayer?
It is one of His best gifts! He longs for you
to receive this special gift from Him.

Could the reading of this book become a spiritual marker in your life? A time of transformation into becoming more like Jesus, of discovery or rediscovery of what it means to live a Christ following life—a day-by-day journey of real spirituality?

I continue to search my own heart and soul and ask the Father to reveal to me those places of need in my life and relationships—with Him and with others.

My prayerful desire is to share in the pages ahead some of the biblical essentials—the pathways—leading to the goal of growing in Christlikeness as we pursue the depths of God. Even as I write, I ask the Father to implant these essentials deep within my own being—beneath the waterline of my life—and yours.

CREATING BALLAST
FOR YOUR LIFE

"Come to me with your ears wide open.
Listen, for the life of your soul is at stake."
—Isaiah 55:3 TLB

I want to begin our quest with a parable—a story of a foolish man who built a boat. The man's intention was that his boat would be the grandest, most talked-about craft ever to sail from the harbor of the boat club of which he was a member. He determined to spare no expense or effort.

He made his plans. The foolish man would outfit his craft with the best of everything—every detail would be beautiful and impressive. And on the bow, in gold letters, he would put the name of the boat, the *Persona*.

He began building the boat, outfitting his craft in color-ful sails, complex rigging, and comfortable appointments and conveniences in the cabin. The decks were made from lovely teakwood; all the fittings were custom-made of polished brass.

One day, it occurred to him: "Why should I spend money or time on what is out of everyone's sight? When I lis-ten to the conversations of people at the club, I can never remember anyone admiring the *underside* of any boat." So the man decided he was not concerned about the boat's keel or ballast or anything that had to do with the matter of properly distributed weight. The seaworthiness of the vessel did not seem an important issue while there in dry dock.

Driven by his reasoning, the foolish man continued his work. Everything visible on the boat soon began to gleam with excellence. However, the foolish man generally ignored those matters that would not be visible when the boat entered the water. As he built the *Persona*, the man could not resist fantasizing about the anticipated admiration and applause of the club members at the launching of his new boat.

The day came for the boat's maiden voyage. The club members joined him at dockside. The traditional bottle was broken over the bow. As he stood proudly at the helm, the man heard what he had anticipated for years: the cheers of the club members. Then, at last, he heard those words so sweet to his ears: "Our club has never seen a grander boat than this one." It was time for the *Persona's* maiden voyage.

The breeze filled the sails and pushed the *Persona* and the foolish man from the club's harbor and then out beyond the breakwater and into the ocean. But a few miles out to sea, a storm arose. The wind and waves became inordinately strong and high. Within minutes, they took their toll on the sails and mast and rigging. And then a wave bigger than anything the man had ever seen crashed down upon the *Persona*, and the boat capsized.

Now this is important! Sailboats are built to right themselves after such a battering, but the *Persona* did not. Why? Because its builder had ignored the importance of what was below the waterline. There was no weight there. A well-designed keel and adequate ballast could have saved the ship, but the foolish man had concerned himself with the *appearance* of things and not with resilience and stability in the secret unseen places where storms are withstood. The foolish man was lost at sea.

The wreckage of the boat washed ashore, ironically, at the boat club. The drowned man's boat club friends gathered around the wreckage in shock and said, "Only a fool would build a boat like this. Surely he knew that in order not to capsize, there must be more weight *below* the waterline than above." However, the boat had been built for the vanity of its builder and for the praise of the spectators. The foolish man is remembered now simply as "the foolish man." (Adapted from *The Life God Blesses* by Gordon McDonald.)

You probably recognize that this parable is about a most significant dimension of our beings—the inner place beneath the waterline of our lives. I use the words "soul" and "heart" interchangeably to refer to this inner aspect of our total beings. All too often, this immortal, essential part of ourselves is neglected. Yet our interior lives—our own depths—have special need of focused attention, for this dimension is an inherent part of who we are. Even active, involved Christians can neglect their inner journeys. Sometimes Christians—especially active, involved Christians—neglect this crucial part of themselves. Indeed, we can be in church every Sunday, we can be Bible teachers, deacons, elders, pastors—even writers of Christian books (help!)—and largely ignore this essential part of who we are.

Dallas Willard, in his book *The Renovation of the Heart,* tells of a time when Mahatma Gandhi was in Great Britain. While there, Gandhi looked closely at Christianity as practiced by "believers" around him. Then he remarked that if only Christians would live according to their belief in the teachings of Jesus, "We would all become Christians."

Frankly, I feel convicted by Gandhi's comment. Too often, I have not *lived* my belief in Jesus' teachings...and this brings into question the authenticity of my belief in my "beliefs."

In other words, *knowing* the right beliefs does not automatically mean that we Christians actually *believe* them! To *believe* the teachings of Jesus would mean the believer would *live them out in observable ways* in the midst of everyday life and relationships. This would be a genuine demonstration of spiritual maturity.

Willard further comments, "Perhaps the hardest thing for sincere Christians to come to grips with is the level of real unbelief in their own lives—the unformulated skepticism about Jesus that permeates all dimensions of their beings and undermines what efforts they do make toward Christlikeness." Unfortunately, what we often reveal in our daily living is our *un*belief, and thus, our failure to become increasingly like Christ.

Pathways to Authentic Faith

I am very practical. Questions come to my mind. What are the non-negotiable *essential* beliefs of the Christ-following life? How do the qualities of *Christlikeness* develop and grow within us? How can we be faithful and consistent in the long-term accumulation of Christ-following responses to life's daily challenges? Are there dependable pathways we can take that, when incorporated into our inner beings and *also* into our lifestyles, will nourish and feed our souls and, at the same time, stabilize us and free us to live authentically and joyfully for God and others?

In these pages, I will seek to surface some responses to these questions and remind you of some old, familiar truths from God's Word. Frankly, I wish I knew some brilliant, dazzling *new* truths to call to your attention, but I don't. I am aware, from my own experiences, that discovering *new* truths with "old" eyes is indeed exciting. However, I have also found that seeing *old* truths with "new" eyes can be just as thrilling! Even as I write these words, I am praying this will happen to you, and to me, as well.

My intention is to open my own life to you—as a fellow struggler, a learner, an unashamed follower of our Lord Jesus Christ. Just as I am, I come to share with you from my own journey with the Father—to reveal my heart and life and my simple, uncomplicated understandings from His profound and trustworthy Word. These basic, non-negotiable essentials, these familiar "pathways" ahead, can be absolutely transforming and growth producing, but only when they become a part of the structure of one's total life. Our adventure involves discovering them again with "new" eyes—even as we place our lives before God, all over again, as an offering. This is our quest, our journey into the depths of God.

"Take your everyday, ordinary life—your sleeping, eating, going-to-work, and walking-around life—and place it before God as an offering."

—Romans 12:1 *The Message*

When a Storm Comes

Probably, many of us tend to lose sight of this below-the-waterline part of our lives. In the midst of our neglect, what breaks in upon us and gets our attention? The parable reminds us that often it is an unexpected storm. When a storm comes and our "boat" rocks, then life itself demands that we look into our inner beings and give attention to those matters deep within, beneath the surface of our visible selves. Have you built within your life spiritual ballast to see you through life's storms?

One thing is certain: we all experience storms. I have experienced several devastating storms and many smaller ones. No one is exempt. Very likely, some of you reading this page are even now in the midst of a wrenching storm. Almost all of us see dark clouds on the horizon that *could* bring disturbances into our experiences.

Storms come in many forms: the death of someone we love, the breakdown of an important relationship, financial pressures, health problems, a deep disappointment in a person or situation, betrayal, broken promises, depression, the resurfacing of painful, unresolved experiences from the past—there are endless forms of disruptive storms. Indeed, we all sooner or later become intimately "acquainted with grief."

Storms are disturbing. They make us feel anxious and remind us how out of our control the elements of life can become. At times a storm will fail to subside, and will rage on and on. We become weary and fatigued. Needs seem to be everywhere we turn, including inside us. Our concern for others nosedives. We may discover we no longer *want* to serve others or witness about Jesus. In fact, in the midst of our own frustration, despair, and heartache, we wonder what there is to bear witness about. In short, storms can attack our inner beings and seriously disrupt our lives. Thus, it is imperative for us to develop spiritual ballast to right the ship of our lives when storms suddenly appear.

Paul Tournier was a Swiss psychiatrist whose books, through the years, have been influential in my life. Dr. Tournier, a deeply devoted Christ follower, spent his life intensely involved with people who were dealing with storms in their lives. He had storms in his own life, and he talked and wrote about them freely in the midst of sharing in the suffering of those who came to him for help. Tournier observed that while some people experience transforming growth through storms and suffering, unfortunately, others are destroyed by them. Wherein lies the difference? His observation was a sobering reminder that the difference is made by one's openness to allowing God to be redemptively at work—loving us, guiding us, sustaining us, growing us, deepening us—in the midst of life's stormy (as well as "unstormy") experiences.

Yes, questions surface throughout our lives. The answers are found in the Word of God, and have to do with the Father's gradual, loving, prodding transformation of our total lives, and thus transformation of our everyday walk and relationships with Him and others. The answers invariably relate to certain "pathways" to spiritual development. They have to do with how our lives, when we cooperate with God's relentless love and grace, can imperceptibly, increasingly become a quiet demonstration of how a faithful follower of Christ lives one's life on planet earth. This is our quest, our search, our journey.

*P*ause and think of a storm you have experienced
in your life. What was your response?

At this point, how would you rate
your growth into Christlikeness?

How can you open yourself to God's
transformation of your inner being in the midst
of the inevitable stormy experiences of life?

How can you be re-formed, reconstructed,
redeemed, not only for your own welfare,
but for the sake of God's kingdom, for the
purpose of becoming Christlike? How can you
be involved in serving God by serving others?

Are you developing spiritual ballast
beneath the waterline of your life?

Read on, my friend, *"for the life of your soul is at stake"* (Isaiah 55:3 TLB).

"Men and women of deep souls, who have weight below the waterline, do not need to talk about life at soul level. It becomes a healthy secret between them and God. The evidence that such life is going on will be seen at stormtime when they ride out the waves while others are capsizing.... 'Mary kept these things and pondered them in her heart' (Luke 2:19)—these are the words of one who doesn't need to tell everyone what is happening at soul-level."

—Gordon MacDonald

PURSUE TRANSFORMATION
INTO CHRISTLIKENESS

"God knew what he was doing from the very beginning.
He decided from the outset to shape the lives of those
who love him along the same lines as the life of his Son....
We see the original and intended shape of our lives there in him."
—Romans 8:29 *The Message*

Deep within us is a desire for *transformation*. The word has a magnetic attraction. We count calories and join health clubs and gyms in order to experience transformation of our bodies. Many of us are attracted to books and conferences in the hope of transforming our thinking, skills, and actions. Even as I write this, we are celebrating the beginning of a new year. My friends and I have had discussions of changes we would like to make in our lives, sharing our resolutions (for however long they may last!) for making those alterations that, hopefully, will bring the form of transformation we desire.

Of course, we are aware that *spiritual* transformation does not take place as a result of New Year's resolutions, or conferences, or reading books. In fact, the very culture in which we live runs decidedly counter to the process of transformation into Christlikeness.

Made to Be Like Jesus

Simply and profoundly, transformation into Christlikeness is God's plan for His people. Indeed, God revealed in the first chapter of the creation account that we are created to be like Jesus.

"Then God said, 'Let us make man in our image, in our likeness.'"
—Genesis 1:26

To be created in the image of God and His Son is one of the most incredible thoughts in the Bible and in the universe! Do we realize what this Scripture is proclaiming? Nothing gives us more worth and dignity than being made in His image.

Is Christlikeness the ultimate goal and desire of your life? Paul's urging reinforces the significance of this matter:

"Take on an entirely new way of life—a God-fashioned life, a life renewed from the inside and working itself into your conduct as God accurately reproduces his character in you."
—Ephesians 4:22b–24 *The Message*

How does this entirely new God-fashioned life come into being?

The Beginning Point: Conversion

Let us acknowledge a basic fact. Before transformation into Christlikeness can even begin to take place, conversion must be experienced. We can only know for ourselves that a total-being relationship has been established with Jesus. In the simplest terms, conversion involves the awareness of our lostness and need of a Savior, our acceptance that Jesus is the One who came in love to give Himself for our costly, forever salvation. This crucial experience of trusting Jesus as one's personal Savior and Lord, humbly repenting, contritely confessing and asking His forgiveness for our sins, accepting His sacrifice on the cross as payment in our stead, and surrendering to His Way for the living of our lives means that conversion itself is immediate, instantaneous.

Yet we know that conversion is only the beginning of life in Christ. Transformation into Christlikeness is the all-important part of the quest. However, this journey (and conversion itself) involves one's entire lifetime.

The First Day of Forever

The transformation process—entrance into a vibrant relationship with the living, reigning Christ—ideally begins immediately upon conversion. Indeed, conversion is the first day of "forever." A steady growth toward Christlikeness from this point on is God's design, desire, and ideal.

*Ideally, the new convert will
be led by a Christ follower
to say to Jesus sincerely,
"Lord, this is the way I am now.
Now, how can I
become like You?"*

39

The Heart of Christlikeness

"In light of all this, here's what I want you to do....I want you to get out there and walk—better yet, run!—on the road God called you to travel. I don't want any of you sitting around on your hands. I don't want anyone strolling off, down some path that goes nowhere."

—Ephesians 4:1 *The Message*

If I were to choose one emphasis to represent most completely the quest of the Christ follower, this chapter captures it. There are many non-negotiable essentials that are significant to our journey, and we will acknowledge them as pathways to our goal.

However, Christlikeness is more than a pathway. Christlikeness is the *venture* and the *mission* of every Christ follower. Until we submit ourselves to this serious renovation of our hearts, we are missing out on the Christ follower's most life-changing, life-challenging experience. Surrendering to this, His way for the living of our days, provides meaning and divine resources for abundant life on this earth here and now.

Ask Jesus to Be Your Daily Teacher

Allowing Jesus to be our teacher is a major step toward transformation into Christlikeness. He is the most brilliant, wisest man in all of history. He was, and is, the Master Teacher. Wonder of wonders, we have opportunity to "learn of Him," to be His student, His disciple, His follower.

"Let the words of Christ, in all their richness, live in your hearts and make you wise."

—Colossians 3:16 NLT

"If anyone loves me, he will obey my teaching."

—John 14:23

Simply, but profoundly, we must major on what Jesus' words and teachings mean in our practical daily living. We are to be obedient each day to all He leads us to incorporate into our relationship with Him and others. In fact, Jesus said that those who love Him *will* obey His teachings.

What do your actions reveal about the level of your obedience?

Living His Truth: The Ultimate Goal of Jesus' Teachings

Our challenge is to go beyond merely reading and knowing *about* Jesus' life and teachings. We need to reflect, absorb, *live* His words, and follow His instructions. Jesus knew what He was talking about. His words are ultimate truth. We must deeply believe Him or our decisions and the resulting actions will lead us into violation of His way of life. We do not "happen" into Christlikeness. The journey toward Christlikeness must be intentional. We must give ultimate attention to the *living* of His truths.

Clearly, the Scriptures reveal over and over again that we are to live as Jesus would live if He were in our circumstances. This applies to our behavior, attitudes, perspectives, relationships—everything about our total beings.

Ask for Help

Before dealing with a difficult situation, a troubled relationship, a seemingly impossible dilemma, or any of the many

41

everyday struggles before us, we have the privilege of directly asking the Father to help us discern how the Master Teacher's truths apply—how Jesus would respond in circumstances similar to ours. Plus, we can count on the Holy Spirit to add His resourceful power to assist us in our desire to be Jesus' credible followers. The Holy Spirit is indeed the magnificent and dependable "plus" to help us through the complexities of our life situations.

"Let this mind be in you, which was also in Christ Jesus."
—Philippians 2:5 KJV

The truth is, of course, that we never arrive at full transformation into Christlikeness in this life. We never completely have "His mind." However, for those who enter into this continual pursuit, the journey toward the goal is life's most meaningful quest.

Again, this is our basic challenge—to allow God to fashion our lives into His likeness and accurately reproduce the character of Christ in us—*until Christ is formed in us.* Simply, but profoundly, Jesus wants us to be like Him.

Do you deeply desire to be like Him?
Do you clearly want His transformation,
His distinct changes within you? Look within
your soul as you reflect on these questions.

In His Steps

"To this you were called, because Christ suffered for you, leaving you an example, that you should follow in his steps."
—1 Peter 2:21

The journey to Christlikeness is not a casual journey. It requires our studied attention to the Scriptures and openness to our Heavenly Father's guidance. Also necessary to the journey is our willingness to "make every effort" to grow and deepen in our love for and our treasuring of Christ. (To experience the Bible's exhortation to do this, see Luke 13:24, Romans 14:19, Ephesians 4:3, 2 Peter 1:5–8, and 2 Peter 3:14.)

Also, the Gospels reveal to us many of Jesus' *actions* that inspire us and lead us to increasing change into Christlikeness. Indeed, we must keep His pattern always before us.

Jesus, Our Model

What did Jesus do on earth that the earnest Christ follower can take as a reasonable pattern—and know we are following His example and walking "in His steps"?

~ **Jesus stayed in intimate fellowship with His Father.**
~ **Jesus saw people as living documents and He wrote His signature across their lives.**
~ **Jesus continuously assaulted the barriers of ethnic and gender walls.**
~ **Jesus shared God's truth at every opportunity.**

Christlike Character Traits

It is helpful to be specific as to the Christlike character traits that need to be developing within *us*. We find Jesus' characteristics in the fruit of the Spirit (Galatians 5:22–23), in His teachings in the beatitudes (Matthew 5:1–12), in one of Peter's letters (2 Peter 1:5–8), and in Paul's chapter on love (1 Corinthians 13). These are only a few of the outstanding passages guiding us toward the biblical challenge of Christlikeness. Read them again and again. Ask God to plant them in your heart.

Meditate even now on the following words from Peter's letter. Take them very personally.

"So don't lose a minute in building on what you've been given, complementing your basic faith with good character, spiritual understanding, alert discipline, passionate patience, reverent wonder, warm friendliness, and generous love, each dimension fitting into and developing the others. With these qualities active and growing in your lives, no grass will grow under your feet, no day will pass without its reward as you mature in your experience of our Master Jesus."

—2 Peter 1:5–8 *The Message*

Our Challenge

Again and again, we come back to Jesus' example. We must live accordingly if we are to be true Christ followers. Whatever Jesus did *then*, we must do *now*. Indeed, we must steadily give close attention to His life and activities as revealed in the Scriptures. Our daily challenge is to be engaged in these same activities, and to have His characteristics increasingly become a part of the fabric of our beings.

Is your clear desire to be like Him?

Words of Caution—and a Promise

Just as our culture today does not validate the process of transformation into Christlikeness, the same was true when Paul wrote to the saints in Rome. How timely are his words to us today.

"Don't become so well-adjusted to your culture that you fit into it without even thinking. Instead, fix your attention on God. You'll be changed from the inside out....Unlike the culture around you, always dragging you down to its level of immaturity, God brings the best out of you, develops well-formed maturity in you."

—Romans 12:2 *The Message*

What an on-target warning and yet, at the same time, a wonderful promise. As we keep our attention fixed on God, we have the assurance of continual transformation from the inside out! We can live our lives today in the light of His trustworthy, long-ago, but up-to-date promise.

Transformation Is Not Automatic

The fact is that transformation is not automatically smooth or necessarily ongoing. For some, growth is rapid. For others, transformation has an ebb and flow. For still others, the process of growth may stall, or even stop. If the stalled condition goes on and on, there may be reason for concern about the validity of the conversion experience from the beginning. Unfortunately, some converts steer clear of the transformation process altogether.

As you read in the introduction, I spent a number of years after my childhood conversion doing all the "good, fine church things" without taking steps toward Christlikeness. Yes, I was assured of going to heaven. But abundant life on earth comes from a close relationship with Christ, and by my actions, I kept a certain distance from Him. Not from His church or His people, but from an intimate closeness with Him.

The defining point in jump-starting my growth process took place when I was a young adult in the transformative class on prayer that I described in the introduction. Only then did I come to the disturbing realization that I had not grown beyond a shallow level in my inner being. I was living my life lacking in the resources God makes available through His Holy Spirit. I was a spiritual toddler.

The Growth Journey Begins

Focusing on these discoveries, I began the intentional, awesome journey of seeking to open myself to growth toward Christlikeness—committing myself at a deep level to the process of knowing Him intimately, loving Him wholeheartedly, and desiring to become like Him.

Sadly, I fear too many of us stay close to the place where we "entered" conversion. We can be immersed in the midst of many fine, even outstanding activities in the spiritual realm, without being in the transformation process. Of course, we are not the judge of others' journeys, but we can certainly be aware of our own progress toward Christlikeness—or our lack of progress. We will never achieve the ultimate goal of Christlikeness in this life, but we can be, and need to be, moving toward that goal.

Introducing the Christ Follower

"Then he said to the crowd, 'If any of you wants to be my follower, you must put aside your selfish ambition, shoulder your cross daily, and follow me. If you try to keep your life for yourself, you will lose it. But if you give up your life for me, you will find true life. And how do you benefit if you gain the whole world but lose or forfeit your own soul in the process?'"

—Luke 9:23–25 NLT

The term "Christ follower" has not always been a part of my

vocabulary. Gordon MacDonald is a prolific author who introduced me to the term. The two simple, profound words resonated deep within me. The idea of being a Christ follower snagged my own soul, and lodged there. I have reflected much on the concept.

I have found myself increasingly using the term *Christ follower* instead of Christian. Originally, the word Christian had such a wonderful meaning. It indicated an actual *follower* of Christ, one who literally walked with Jesus as He taught and led those who linked their lives with His, wanting to learn from Him. The word *Christian* indicated, among other shades of meaning, that a person was a "little Christ." It was a way for Jesus' followers to identify themselves ever-so-closely with Him, His teachings, and His call to an extraordinary kind of life.

But "little Christ" is no longer the usual connotation of the word *Christian*. No more do we automatically think of a Christian as a serious learner or close follower of Jesus. Today, in fact, the word *Christian* can have a wide range of definitions that don't necessarily indicate that one is a deeply committed disciple of Christ. It can refer to something that is mostly cultural, or largely a business or political enterprise, or an affiliation with a group—but not a relationship with Jesus. For some time now, I have been using "Christ follower" nearly exclusively when referring to the earnest Christian.

What Does It Mean to Be a Christ Follower?

Simply stated, a Christ follower is one who conscientiously seeks to live a Christlike life, both in the interior of the heart—in terms of one's continual, intimate communion with God in Christ—and in one's outer life of experiences, situations, and relationships. A Christ follower never graduates from learning from Him. It is a lifelong experience.

The authentic Christ follower is in the process of "knowing God." James I. Packer has written the book *Knowing God*, considered by many a classic in this important field of understanding. Packer insists that God is to be *known* and not merely *known about*. He makes a distinction between knowing God "by description" and knowing Him "by acquaintance." He further writes,

> What matters supremely, therefore, is not, to the last analysis, the fact that I know God, but the larger fact which underlies it—the fact that he knows me. I am graven on the palm of his hands. I am never out of his mind...there is never a moment when his eye is off me, or his attention distracted from me, and no moment, therefore, when his care falters.
>
> This is momentous knowledge. There is unspeakable comfort...in knowing that God is constantly taking care of me in love, and watching over me for my good. There is tremendous relief in knowing that his love for me is utterly realistic, based at every point on prior knowledge of the worst about me, so that no discovery now can disillusion him about me.
>
> —J. I. Packer, *Knowing God*

Thus, the primary goal of the maturing Christ-following life is to be in the process of knowing God and becoming more and more like Jesus. Simply and profoundly, *transformation into Christlikeness* is God's plan for His people. In His Word, He has given us pathways that lead to the realization of this life-changing, life-enhancing goal. The remainder of this book will involve an invitation to walk together down these pathways to Christlikeness. On these pathways we will pursue the depths of God.

pathway one

SHIFT YOUR FOCUS
TO THE
SPIRITUAL REALM

"From now on you must grow stronger through union with the Lord and through His mighty power. You must put on God's full armor, so as to be able to stand up against the devil's stratagems. For our contest is not with human foes alone, but with the rulers, authorities, and cosmic powers of this dark world; that is, with the spirit-forces of evil challenging us in the heavenly contest. So you must take on God's full armor, so as to be able to take a stand in the day when evil attacks you, and after having completely finished the contest, to hold your own. Hold your position, then, with your waist encircled with the belt of truth, put on right-doing as a coat of mail, and put on your feet the preparation, the good news of

peace supplies. Besides all these, take on the shield which faith provides, for with it you will be able to put out all the fire-tipped arrows shot by the evil one, take the helmet salvation provides, and take the sword the Spirit wields, which is the word of God. Keep on praying in the Spirit, with every kind of prayer and entreaty, at every opportunity, be ever on the alert with perfect devotion and entreaty for all God's people, and for me that a message may be given me when I open my lips, so that I may boldly make known the open secret of the good news…so that…I may speak as courageously as I ought."

—Ephesians 6:10–20 (Williams)

*P*aul here draws our attention absolutely to the spiritual realm. He is reminding us that life becomes a constant warfare between good and evil for the Christ follower. Unless we recognize that fact and become proactive in our preparations for the battle, we can easily be defeated in the most important spiritual struggle we will ever encounter.

We are reminded everywhere we turn that "spiritual" is a very trendy word today. Our world is "into" spirituality. We hear and see these words related to health, ballet, sports, best-selling books, morning talk shows, magazines, television, and billboard ads. "Spirituality" is fashionable. In a George Barna survey in 2003, 92% of Americans claimed to be "spiritual."

If we stay on the surface of life's activities, events, and relationships, we will deal with only those matters that are visible and outward, above the waterline. We *must* give insightful attention to the below-the-waterline part of our lives. We must go into the interior, the deepest part of ourselves, where no one but God can see or know or touch. Each of us needs to go regularly into the Holy of Holies and look within our hearts, our souls. We must shift our focus to the spiritual realm on our pathway toward Christlikeness.

This is where, when we allow Him to, God draws us to Himself in intimacy, and then toward others in love. This is where, when we open our beings to Him, He heals our wounds, imparts hope, courage, endurance, and stability, and implants His convictions and His perspective within. If this happens at all, it happens deep inside.

Of course, there are always some (perhaps many) who want their private selves to be left alone. They prefer to live their lives without sobering thoughts of what is beneath the waterline. Then when a storm comes and the boat rocks, life itself shouts out to them, and to each of us, to look within. There comes the moment of truth about the condition of our walk with God, the reality of our spiritual focus, the authenticity of our Christ following, and the state of our Christlikeness.

As we seek to shift our focus to the spiritual realm, let us come to further understanding of the word *spiritual*. The philosopher Demosthenes said, "Wisdom begins with definition." Can spirituality be adequately defined? Like love, a definition of spirituality is difficult to put into mere words. Nevertheless, let us make our way through the verbal debris, and try for an adequate description. Sometimes we gain needed light when we state first what a definition is *not*, and then define what it *is*.

To focus on the spiritual realm is *not* using spiritual sounding "God talk," words that appear and sound religious, even pious, but are not an integral part of one's heart, soul, and life. Focusing on the spiritual realm is *not* looking intently within in order to get in touch with one's higher self. It is *not* going through the motions of the spiritual disciplines. It is *not* keeping the rules without having the relationship (a person can do everything "right" and still be 99% hypocrite).

There are other *nots* we could state, but you get the drift. Then what *does* it mean to focus on the spiritual realm?

Shifting one's focus to the spiritual realm involves God—knowing Him, loving Him, pleasing Him, obeying Him, enjoying Him, worshipping Him, and thus bringing glory to Him. It means intimate commitment to Jesus Christ as the Son of God—to His love, life, teachings, death, resurrection, and redemption. Certainly, the spiritual realm also includes embracing the Holy Spirit—His fruit, gifts, call, and His daily empowerment. It requires obedience to God's Word, the Bible—reading it, knowing it, absorbing it, and *living* the Scriptures. Spiritual nourishment must be further enhanced through reading not only the Bible, but also other challenging, inspirational, insightful books and articles. The spiritual realm's most consistent theme is love; the greatest commandment—loving God with all one's heart, mind, soul, and strength, as well as loving and serving one's neighbor, and others as oneself.

How can we tell if one is living with a focus on the spiritual realm? Their attitudes and activities are rooted in the person of Jesus Christ, His words and His work, especially as revealed in the New Testament. Hallmarks of this spirituality are faith, hope, and again, above all, love—God's love as demonstrated in the life of Jesus and His followers. His love does not stipulate a way of doing certain things. It requires a certain way of doing *everything*—the way of love. Shifting our focus to the spiritual realm calls us to be devoted followers of Christ, and daily *doing* Christlike things, living "in His steps."

Today's thirst for spiritual things reveals a deep longing in the human soul for more than meets the eye. Our personal responsibility as Christ followers is to help satisfy that longing as we point others to the One who can meet that deep need.

pathway two

DEVELOP AN ACCURATE PICTURE OF GOD

"God is love. When we take up permanent residence in a life of love, we live in God and God lives in us. This way, love has the run of the house, becomes at home and mature in us."

—1 John 4:16–17 *The Message*

"He [Jesus] is the image of the invisible God....For God was pleased to have all his fullness dwell in him."

—Colossians 1:15, 19

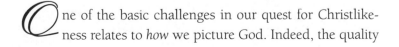ne of the basic challenges in our quest for Christlikeness relates to *how* we picture God. Indeed, the quality

of our Christ following and the way we live our lives depends on the accuracy of our understanding of God. What is God like?

God is beyond our finite comprehension. We are keenly aware that we do not have the ability to fully comprehend Him. We finite human beings can never, ever begin to grasp all that He is. Yet *how* we live our lives comes from *how* we picture God, and what we believe about Him. If our picture of God is distorted, the fallout takes its toll on our perspectives, attitudes, and relationships. We *must* have an accurate picture of God, or our lives will be hopelessly and endlessly askew. This is an essential pathway to Christlikeness.

What Is Your Picture of God?

Sometimes I feel sorry for God, because He gets blamed for so many things that are tragic, or traumatic, or evil, or the result of our violations of His will, or our dumb choices. We live in an imperfect world with imperfect people committing imperfect actions. Our loving Father does not *will* awful things. His perfect will is not death and destruction from accidents or storms. (I am reminded of insurance companies describing natural disasters as "acts of God." I disagree with their theology!) Neither is it His perfect will for terrorists to crash planes into buildings, killing thousands of innocent people, nor for students to be shot at school or church by fellow students, nor for those we love to die prematurely. What a distorted picture of God this would be.

To Know the Father, Turn to His Son

The most reliable place to go for the most authentic understanding of God is directly to Jesus. Our Master Teacher taught us about God in the parable of the prodigal son (Luke 15). We are almost too familiar with the story, for we can easily rush right past the moving, accurate picture Jesus is giving us of His, and our, Heavenly Father.

You know the story. The younger son violated his father's love and asked for his inheritance, an impudent, outrageous request, especially in a Middle Eastern family. But he said to his father, in essence, "I want right now what's coming to me!" The son took his inheritance and went off to the far country. He "lived it up," spending his money riotously and recklessly.

In due time, his inheritance was gone, and the day came when the son was hungry and desperate. While slopping the pigs he was hired to care for (an especially disgusting job for a Jewish man), he finally came to his senses. In despair, he remembered his dad's hired hands were living in dignity while he labored in squalor and disgrace. He made a dramatic decision and headed for home, rehearsing the confession and repentance he had in his heart.

His return was as dramatic as his departure had been. His father had been searching the horizon daily to see if his wayward son could possibly be coming home. Finally, unbelievably, the father saw in the distance, coming down the road toward home, a familiar walk. Could this be *his* boy?

With his heart pounding, the father ran (can't you just see his robe flying in the wind?) to embrace and kiss his son. The boy started the contrite speech of repentance he had planned to say to his dad upon reaching home. Notice that he only got part of the way through it. "Father, I've sinned against heaven and against you. I am no longer worthy to be called your son," he said (Luke 15:21). That's when the father interrupted him, not even allowing his son to finish what he intended to say, which was, "Father, will you take me on as a hired hand?"

A Father's Extravagant Love

The dad was not listening to his son's confession and plea. He was ecstatically giving instructions to his servants, calling for clean clothes for his son, a ring, sandals, a feast, dancing, and a huge celebration. That's what God is like. More than a parable of a prodigal son, this is a parable of a father's extravagant love. *This story gives us an accurate portrait of God!*

But then the story becomes increasingly complex. The elder son entered, bitter and resentful. He said to the father, his words dripping with sarcasm and hurt, "You never threw a big celebration for *me*, and I have been here all along." The father said one of the sweetest statements in all the Bible. He replied, *"Son, everything I have is yours."*

That's what God is like! He makes *all* His resources available to His children.

At times we have been the rebellious prodigal, going our own way. At times we have been the elder brother, doing the right thing above the waterline, but resentful and jealous below the waterline, failing the opportunity for Christlikeness. Perhaps the deepest, most challenging truth is that there are times when, as Henri Nouwen pointed out, we are called upon to *be the father*, to be the one who loves extravagantly, forgivingly—and then lovingly, eagerly welcomes back the prodigal into his heart and home.

This parable reminds us of our own times of rebellion and our need to return in brokenness to the Father's open arms. We must remember that *we* have been the prodigal—each of us—we have sinned! Perhaps we are living as a prodigal right now and need to come to the place of brokenness and repentance before our loving, forgiving Father.

The parable could also represent times when our love has been shunned by persons close to us, and we suffer. Again, this is not the final chapter. Everything that happens, God knows is coming. Thus, He is creatively, passionately, and powerfully at work at *all* times, within us and all around us, to whatever degree we will allow Him to be, teaching us, refining us, deepening us. He brings into our lives, time and again, what Trevor Hudson, in his book *Christ-Following*, calls "little Easters."

God's "Little Easters"

God is the author and director of the first Easter—history's most momentous event. In His love, the Father continues to bring little Easters into our lives. What is a little Easter? Hudson defines a little Easter as "just about anytime we are surprised with new possibilities for life and healing in the midst of brokenness and decay."

Indeed, God specializes in bringing little Easters into our experiences. Paul divinely documents this truth, and gives us an accurate picture of God's care: "That's why we can be so sure that every detail in our lives of love for God is worked into something good" (Romans 8:28 *The Message*). God will bring good out of literally everything that comes our way. We have His Word! Therefore, I am confident that the day will come when we will see and understand how He has used all of our experiences to fashion us into Christlikeness.

With Paul, we can be certain that God *is* at work within us and all around us in every situation. Even in times we do not understand, we can have confidence that His love for us is total and unconditional. He is completely worthy of our trust, a magnificent fact to be embedded deep within our heart of hearts at all times and places.

My picture of God in this regard is that He does not *cause* the airplane crash. God does not plan and bring cancer to a certain person at a certain time and place. He does not reach down in the middle of a late Sunday night and personally zap a heart to stop its beating. Of course, He knows these experiences are coming. In ways we recognize only in retrospect, He sensitively prepares us for them, just as He continues to be at work, ministering faithfully to His people, both in the midst of, and in the aftermath of life's storms.

Please remember there are many situations we cannot now, nor will we ever in this life on earth, be able to explain.

"'My thoughts are completely different from yours,' says the LORD. *'And my ways are far beyond anything you could imagine. For just as the heavens are higher than the earth, so are my ways higher than your ways and my thoughts higher than your thoughts.'"*
—Isaiah 55:8–9 (NLT)

Here are a few Scriptures that give us some attributes describing what God is like.

God Is Love
"And so we know and rely on the love God has for us. God is love. Whoever lives in love lives in God, and God in him. In this way, love is made complete among us so that we will have confidence on the day of judgment."
—1 John 4:16–17

"How great is the love the Father has lavished on us, that we should be called children of God! And that is what we are!"
—1 John 3:1

God Is Revealed in Jesus
"He [Jesus] is the image of the invisible God, the firstborn over all creation."
—Colossians 1:15

"The Son is the radiance of God's glory and the exact representation of his being, sustaining all things by his powerful word."

—Hebrews 1:3

God Is Holy

"Holy, holy, holy is the LORD Almighty; the whole earth is full of his glory."

—Isaiah 6:3

"Your ways, O God, are holy."

—Psalm 77:13

God Is Present

"The LORD himself goes before you and will be with you; he will never leave you nor forsake you."

—Deuteronomy 31:8

"Make your home in me just as I do in you."

—John 15:4 (*The Message*)

God Is All-Powerful

"Great is our Lord and mighty in power."

—Psalm 147:5

"His incomparably great power for us who believe."

—Ephesians 1:19

God Forgives

"If we confess our sins, he is faithful and just and will forgive us our sins and purify us from all unrighteousness."
—1 John 1:9

"When you were stuck in your old sin-dead life, you were incapable of responding to God. God brought you alive—right along with

Christ! Think of it! All sins forgiven, the slate wiped clean, that old arrest warrant canceled and nailed to Christ's cross."

—Colossians 2:13–14 *The Message*

God Wants to Shape Us

"And then take on an entirely new way of life—a God-fashioned life, a life renewed from the inside and working itself into your conduct as God accurately reproduces his character in you."

—Ephesians 4:22b–24 *The Message*

God Keeps His Promises

"Through these he has given us his great and very precious promises."

—2 Peter 1:4

"The Lord is not slow in keeping his promise."

—2 Peter 3:9

Reflect on these simple, profound Scriptural statements that portray an accurate picture of God.

Is your picture of God harmonious with these biblical truths?

Augustine said, "God loves each of us as though there were no other to love, and He loves all as He loves each."

Richard Foster wrote, "God does not have favorites, but He does have intimates." God wants us as intimates.

Does the word "intimate" describe your relationship with God?

pathway three

STRIVE FOR TRANSPARENCY IN EVERY AREA OF LIFE

"Since, then, we do not have the excuse of ignorance, every-thing—and I do mean everything—connected with that old way of life has to go. It's rotten through and through. Get rid of it! And then take on an entirely new way of life—a God-fashioned life, a life renewed from the inside and working itself into your conduct as God accurately reproduces his character in you. What this adds up to, then, is this: no more lies, no more pre-tense. Tell your neighbor the truth. In Christ's body we're all connected to each other, after all. When you lie to others, you end up lying to yourself."

—Ephesians 4:22–25 *The Message*

"Let every detail in your lives—words, actions, whatever—be done in the name of the Master, Jesus, thanking God the Father every step of the way."

—Colossians 3:17 *The Message*

*W*hat a ringing call for transparency! Paul the apostle, calling himself a "special agent of Christ Jesus," is writing to the faithful Christ followers in Ephesus and Colosse, and to us. He is so straightforward. Paul challenges them and us to discard every form of pretense and live an entirely new way of life. This different kind of life is renewed from the *inside* by God's Holy Spirit, and then will work its newness into every aspect of our character and conduct. In a nutshell, this is how God reproduces *His* character in us—the goal of every faithful follower of Christ. This is a necessary pathway to Christlikeness.

A Life Goal

The Living Bible paraphrases Ephesians 4:15–16 in a way that has become one of my daily, first-thing-in-the-morning recommitments to the Father. It is a life goal for me, and I personalize the Scripture as my heart turns heavenward:

"[Lord, I will] lovingly follow the truth at all times—speaking truly, dealing truly, living truly—and so become more and more in every way like Christ…"

Like Christ! He was totally transparent and completely sincere. No pretense. No masks. No games. This is also my goal. I will not reach it in this life, but this is my desire.

Like Christ, His followers see the world as it really is— and themselves also as they are. They recognize the ambiguities of life and don't feel the need to explain them away. They walk and live "in the light" (1 John 1:7).

On the other hand, some Christians tend to deny reality and feel compelled to put up a front and explain away tough times and hard knocks—or sweep them under the most convenient rug, as though they don't exist. Transparent Christ followers acknowledge God's supernatural power and do not require dramatic miracles to prove He is real. They have no expectation that He produce magic solutions to their problems. At the same time, they turn to Him for His limitless resources in the difficult situations as well as the everyday negotiations of life.

Jesus is, as always, our example in transparency. He was (and is) lovingly real in every area of life. Underline "lovingly." And also "real." This is how we, too, are to come to God and to others.

Dealing with the Truth

What does it mean to be a transparent Christ follower in daily life? We will seek to answer this question in a number of (path) ways. This pathway focuses on living the truth in our daily lives. We are to:

~ courageously tell ourselves the real truth
~ lovingly tell others the truth
~ humbly hear the truth about ourselves

Those are three short, not-always-sweet, but potent points. We are constantly tempted to be less than real, to shade the truth, ignore it, hide it, rationalize it, close our ears to it. Too often, many of us resist *hearing* the truth, especially about ourselves, as well as *telling* the truth, especially when it hurts. It is difficult to be transparent.

I love peace, and I hate conflict. If the truth is unpleasant, I don't want to deal with it. Instinctively, I want to protect myself and others from unpleasantness and hurt. I do not like the relational fall-out after confrontation. These facts make me vulnerable to rationalization. I don't enjoy confessing this, but I can come up with a fairly convincing rationalization for just about anything!

I struggled with this tendency in myself in my relationship with my husband, my children, friends, neighbors, and coworkers. Finally it dawned on me. More accurately, the Father got through to me that while I was smoothing over a situation on the outside, the "inside stuff" was festering beneath the surface. I was not telling myself or others the whole truth. I was not being transparent.

However, I have lived so long now that I can guarantee you (because I have learned, often the hard way) that peace-at-any-price is a counterfeit peace. Peace-at-any-price involves pretense, the wearing of some form of mask. It is true that a mask and the pretense it represents may provide an element of tenuous, *temporary* peace. However, such a "peace" deteriorates the relationship. Eventually, the pretense breaks through—or perhaps I should say the truth breaks through. The unfortunate, bald-faced fact is that non-transparency makes meaningful relationship impossible.

To me, this statement is extremely sobering. I take the truth it expresses very seriously. **Non-transparency does not work!** If non-transparency exists long enough, the relationship eventually dies—a painful inevitability. Some of us, perhaps all of us, have experienced this disappointment in the midst of an important relationship. Twisting matters away from the truth chips away one's selfhood, one's integrity, for we are "to lovingly follow the truth at all times, speaking truly, dealing truly, living truly, and so become more and more like Christ" (Ephesians 4:15–16 TLB).

A Vital Truth

My life was impacted some years ago by a line from one of John Powell's little books, titled *Why Am I Afraid to Tell You Who I Am?* He wrote: "The most loving thing I can give you is the truth."

This statement resonated with me. It was a freeing fact—so simple and dependable, but often not applied to day-by-day relationships and situations. Embracing this truth and seeking to integrate its simplicity and dynamism into the deepest level of life and relationships was an important spiritual marker for me. I have observed the reality of this principle in action again and again, whether I wanted to see it or not!

Transparency really works!

I am *not* recommending being compulsive in saying everything we know and think and believe to be true and real—to everyone. We must never be brutal. On the other hand, we must be wise. Transparency requires integrity, character, courage, and kindness to be *lovingly* forthright even when it is difficult to be so—*especially* when it is difficult to be so. We must be attuned to God's loving wisdom and leading, or we will do more harm than good. This requires "consecrated common sense."

Don't Violate the Truth

If you are in a relationship where you are not lovingly telling the truth, you are withholding thoughts and feelings vital to the integrity of the relationship—there is not authentic communion. Truth is being violated. Christ following does not happen without our intentional, consistent, daily attention and recommitment to realness in the very depths of our relationships, attitudes, decisions, priorities, appearances, and words.

Another aspect of transparency in everyday life has to do with another of life's significant questions: Down deep, whom do we *most* want to please? Is it God, some person or group, or ourselves?

Jesus' teachings in the Sermon on the Mount give us a blueprint. Compare His insightful words in the New International Version and the contemporary rendering of *The Message* as Jesus emphasizes that our acts of service should be done without desiring recognition. He said it best:

"Be careful not to do your 'acts of righteousness' before men, to be seen by them. If you do, you will have no reward from your Father in heaven.

"So when you give to the needy, do not announce it with trumpets, as the hypocrites do in the synagogues and on the streets, to be honored by men. I tell you the truth, they have received their reward in full. But when you give to the needy, do not let your left hand know what your right hand is doing, so that your giving may be in secret. Then your Father, who sees what is done in secret, will reward you."

—Matthew 6:1–4 NIV

"Be especially careful when you are trying to be good so that you don't make a performance out of it. It might be good theater, but the God who made you won't be applauding.

"When you do something for someone else, don't call attention to yourself. You've seen them in action, I'm sure—'playactors' I call them—treating prayer meeting and street corner alike as a stage, acting compassionate as long as someone is watching,

playing to the crowds. They get applause, true, but that's all they get. When you help someone out, don't think about how it looks. Just do it—quietly and unobtrusively."
—Matthew 6:1–4 *The Message*

Jesus applies this same warning about "playacting" to the experience of prayer.

"And when you come before God, don't turn that into a theatrical production either. All these people making a regular show out of their prayers, hoping for stardom! Do you think God sits in a box seat?"
—Matthew 6:5 *The Message*

Jesus is such a clear communicator. He tells His hearers (including us) clearly what He wants His people to be and to do. He wants us to find a secluded place for prayer so we won't be tempted to role-play before God. He continued: "Just be there as simply and honestly as you can manage." He promised, "The focus will shift from you to God, and you will begin to sense His grace" (Matthew 6:6 *The Message*).

In words we should never forget, Jesus taught us what prayer should be.

"The world is full of so-called prayer warriors who are prayer-ignorant. They're full of formulas and programs and advice, peddling techniques for getting what you want from God. Don't fall for that nonsense. This is your Father you are dealing with, and he knows better than you what you need. With a God like this loving you, you can pray very simply. Like this:

Our Father in heaven,
Reveal who you are.

Set the world right;
Do what's best—
As above, so below.
Keep us alive with three square meals,
Keep us forgiven with you and forgiving others.
Keep us safe from ourselves and the Devil.
You're in charge!
You can do anything you want!
You're ablaze in beauty!
Yes. Yes. Yes."

—Matthew 6: 7–15 *The Message*

The simple, profound point of this pathway is: be lovingly real in every aspect of life. Can you sincerely pray this prayer?

Lord of reality
make me real
not plastic
synthetic
pretend phony
an actor playing out his part
hypocrite.
I don't want to keep a prayer list
but to pray.
I don't want to agonize to find Your will
but to obey what I already know.
Help me not to argue theories of inspiration
but to submit to Your word.
I don't want to explain the difference
between *eros* and *agape*
but to love.
I don't want to sing as if I mean it.
I want to mean it.

I don't want to tell it like it is
but to be it like You want it.

> —From *Psalms of My Life*, by Joseph Bayly
> (Wheaton, IL: Tyndale House, 1969)

"Let every detail in your lives—words, actions, whatever—be done in the name of the Master, Jesus, thanking God the Father every step of the way."

> —Colossians 3:17 *The Message*

"If godliness is not from deep within you, it is only a mask."

> —Jeanne Guyon

"Character is what you are in the dark." —Dwight L. Moody

"Almost all our faults are preferable to the methods we resort to in attempting to hide them."

> —Francois de la Rochefoucauld

pathway four

INCORPORATE
SPIRITUAL DISCIPLINES
INTO YOUR DAILY LIFE

"Exercise daily in God—no spiritual flabbiness, please! Workouts in the gymnasium are useful, but a disciplined life in God is far more so, making you fit both today and forever. You can count on this. Take it to heart."

—1 Timothy 4:7–9 *The Message*

With Jesus as our daily teacher, He modeled for us the necessity of incorporating spiritual disciplines into our daily lives. Indeed, spiritual disciplines are essential for growing into Christlikeness. In another translation of the verse above, Paul wrote to Timothy, his "son in the faith":

"Take time and trouble to keep yourself spiritually fit. Bodily fitness has a certain value, but spiritual fitness is essential, both for this present life and for the life to come."

—1 Timothy 4:7–8 (Phillips)

Scripture insists that discipline is essential for the spiritual health of the Christ follower. However, spiritual fitness is not an easy matter to negotiate, for it requires time, effort, and focus. Our hectic schedules do not lend themselves to faithful involvement with spiritual disciplines. Even when we pause, inwardly we keep whirling. I am sobered by the words of Corrie ten Boom: "Beware the barrenness of a busy life." Henry Nouwen observed: "Our lives are filled, yet unfulfilled." Vance Havner wrote: "The alternative to discipline is disaster." And I say from my experience: Without discipline, I recycle my frustrations and stifle the sound of God's still, small voice within.

Just think of all the expectations confronting the serious Christ follower. We *need* to read the Bible daily, as well as give ourselves to regular in-depth Bible study. We *ought* to pray systematically, and also without ceasing. (This does not mean that we are to go around muttering words to God at all times. It means that we are to *live* in such a way that there is no difference in us when we are on our knees and when we go about our daily living.) There are expectations that we memorize Scripture, meditate, fellowship with believers, witness to unbelievers, give to missions, love our spouse, love and train our children, exercise our gifts, journal our inner thoughts, manage our finances. And we find ourselves weary before we even begin to give attention to the oughts and needs and expectations of the disciplines.

You will not be surprised as I share with you that I do not even like the word *discipline*. As I told you in the introduction, during my childhood, discipline was synonymous with peach tree switches!

Discipline is not easy for me, but I embrace it fully for I have learned, often the hard way, that I must respect its requirements in order to receive its benefits. The Bible assures me this is so—and so does life. Indeed, the Christ-following disciplines help us in our desire to live life as Jesus, our teacher, modeled and taught us. I welcome them.

"Spiritual discipline allows us to place ourselves before God so he can speak to us."

—Richard Foster

"Spiritual discipline is the effort to create some space in which God can work."

—Henri Nouwen

"The things that matter most must never be at the mercy of the things that matter least."

—Goethe

What do you suggest should be the first discipline to acknowledge? As I have raised this question in group discussions, usually the first suggestion is "prayer." But I am not going to begin with "prayer." I believe the beginning point needs to be...

The Discipline of Simplicity. I am placing simplicity first because most of us need to simplify our lives before we will have time or space for the other disciplines of the spiritual life. In the midst of all the complexities of our days, we must *unclutter our lives.*

Let me ask you to take a brief reality check: Do you have too much *stuff* in your closet? In your billfold? Your desk? Your computer? Your freezer? I do.

How about your heart? Do you have so much clutter in your heart that you don't have room for devotion to Christ and the other essentials of the Christ-following life?

God is calling us to *reorder* our lives. The discipline of simplicity is a non-negotiable essential, for this discipline frees us for including the other disciplines into our hectic schedules. Write down "Simplify" and keep it before you as a daily reminder. Simplicity is one of those roads less traveled. We *must* reorder our lives. Let us give attention to other basic, familiar disciplines necessary for growing toward Christlikeness.

The Discipline of Time in the Word of God. The basic discipline of ongoing study of the Word of God needs to be a daily experience in the life of the Christ follower. I frequently remind myself that the further step is to add the *application* of the Word of God to my life. The apostle James was one who was insistent on this point. Indeed, this discipline is basic for the Christ follower and splashes over into *all* the pathways to Christlikeness.

The Discipline of Solitude with the Lord. Jesus said, "When you pray, go away by yourself, shut the door behind you, and pray to your Father secretly" (Matthew 6:6 NLT). This discipline is frequently acknowledged as important, but difficult to observe faithfully. I believe the time for daily solitude with the Father needs to take place with respect for each one's personal timing, schedule, and temperament. I am not one who insists the daily quiet time must be experienced in the early morning like the biblical folks and the saints (and many respected writers) observed themselves and recommend to us. Instead, I place an emphasis on giving the Father our "prime time," when we are at our best and most alert. For me, "prime time" is definitely not in the early morning! Since God's prime time is 24/7, I have become convinced that He welcomes our attention at *any* time, but perhaps enjoys us most when we are most alert to His presence and guidance.

The goals of the solitude are: (1) To know God more intimately, to love and worship Him increasingly, and to become more like Jesus. (2) To intercede for others, especially to pray for matters that are God's heart's desire—His prayer requests of us. Yes, He does have prayer requests! His ultimate request is that we pray for people of all nations to come to know and love His Son.

I urge every Christ follower to create, under our Lord's guidance, a personal prayer strategy for regularly spending quality time with Him. This time needs to include praying for *His* heart's desires, as well as our own.

Generally, times of solitude or quiet time are more meaningful when there is a reasonable, flexible structure to follow. Many include the traditional ACTS of prayer. I continue to find them helpful. However, I add another "S" for surrender and an "L" for listening (ACTSSL). Let's go over them together.

A doration—worship and praise of God; focusing on His nature and character

C onfession—repenting and naming our sins; grieving with God about them

T hanksgiving—praising the Lord as the source of every good gift

S upplication—asking for specific matters for ourselves and for others

S urrender—expressing our yielding to God's will: "Thy will, not mine, be done."

L istening—for God's still, quiet voice and hearing His voice in His Word.

The Discipline of Listening. I believe God is always speaking to us. Are you regularly listening for His voice? There is an old Indian adage that came to my attention years ago: "Listen, or thy tongue will make thee deaf." In our time with God, we are prone to do all the talking. Too often, when we get through expressing all we have on our hearts and in our minds, we tend to consider our time with the Father complete, and we are off and gone! We fail to be still and quiet and hear what He is saying to us. Too often, we say, in essence, "Listen, Lord, for your servant is speaking," instead of "Speak, Lord, for your servant is listening!"

I am convinced that listening can revolutionize a relationship, both with God and with people. The need for this discipline cries for our attention every day. We must listen, most urgently to the Father, and very carefully to one another. Listening is our pathway to understanding. How *we* long to be heard and understood! I suspect God has that same longing, also.

The Discipline of Reading. Reading and absorbing meditative, inspirational, challenging books, from the classics, as well as current writers, is another life-changing discipline. There are hundreds from which to choose: Amy Carmichael, Andrew Murray, E. M. Bounds, S. D. Gordon, William Law, Teresa of Avila, Oswald Chambers, C. S. Lewis, Dallas Willard, Richard Foster, T. W. Hunt, Beth Moore, Henry Blackaby, Karla Worley, and Donald Whitney. I challenge you to be reading some soul-feeding materials, in addition to the Bible, that enhance your inner being, challenge your thinking, cause you to become one of the *deep people*, and inspire you to live like Jesus would live if He were in your circumstances.

The Discipline of Reflection. An often-neglected discipline is reflecting and pondering, thinking through issues, conflicts, confusions, paradoxes, and decisions. This relates closely to the discipline of seeking the mind of Christ and His insights in the light of the Scriptures. I believe this discipline must also be considered as a separate and distinct pathway, for reflection is a must in the Christ-following life (see Pathway 12: Think, Reflect, Ponder).

The Discipline of Witness. Delighting in sharing the good news of Jesus in natural, simple, conversational ways in our immediate surroundings and wherever we find ourselves is a discipline we are tempted to take as optional. Yet it is not optional. We are to bear witness of our own personal relationship with God in Christ, to those around us and wherever the Father prompts us to be and to go. He is calling increasing numbers of His people to go "to the ends of the earth" with His message of redemption. However, He is calling *every* Christ follower to be His witness here…now…daily.

The Discipline of Service. Jesus gave special attention to the poor, the lonely, the neglected. I will use a full chapter to discuss this discipline. For now, we acknowledge that serving others is a discipline to which we must give ourselves regularly, naturally, and wholeheartedly, without receiving credit or recognition. The latter part may be the larger discipline! (See Pathway 8: Serve the Lord and Others …With Gladness.)

The Discipline of Priorities. The discipline of priorities is a first cousin to the discipline of simplicity. Some of us claim "Everything I do is priority. *Everything* on my schedule must be done, and I am overwhelmed!" Wait a minute. God does not give us more priorities than we can handle. A priority matter is something *He* intends that we give our attention to.

Our priorities *must* come from God. We can give assent to this statement with good intention, and then our own selfish desires tend to insert themselves into our days as "priorities." I find myself scheduling self-centered priorities whenever I neglect to consult the Father. Are you able to name the Father's priorities for you? This takes us back to the discipline of reflection and listening—we must thoughtfully, prayerfully discern God's custom-designed priorities just for each of us, and schedule *them.*

As a reality check, how many things did you do last week that were not really His priorities, but yours? Frankly, I always need, day by day, to give attention to God's priorities for me for *this* day, and make sure I am spending my time on *them.* This is a major, key discipline and it relates closely to Christ following and authentic, mature spirituality.

The Discipline of Time. The appropriate use of our time is closely akin to the discipline of priorities, and may be the discipline that provokes the most frustration. The many demands that take our time and energy on an average day have a way of keeping us off balance with a hassled feeling of being slightly (and sometimes more than slightly!) overwhelmed. Too often, we spend our precious time, according to the familiar phrase, "greasing the wheel that's squeaking the loudest."

Time is precious. *How* we spend our time is indeed a spiritual matter. Seeking to know God's mind as to the best investment of the time of our lives is rather easy to discuss, but difficult to carry out. Yet the disciplines of time and priorities are key issues of the Christ-following life.

God has wonderfully gifted each of His children with abilities that are to be dedicated to Him, developed in His service, used to further His kingdom, and in it all, bring joy to us.

The Discipline of Stewardship. This discipline deals, not only with the Christ-honoring use of our money, but the disciplined use of our time, opportunities, and God-given gifts. Also included is the stewardship of using well the resources of the Father's creation. Discipline covers every area of life. The discipline of stewardship is intertwined with and impacts all the other disciplines.

The Discipline of Anonymity (Secrecy). In our service to God and people, we are to offer ourselves in ways that do not seek credit and recognition for ourselves. When we do what we do to impress others or to enjoy the attention inherent in the service we offer, we have sacrificed our spiritual authenticity on the altar of self-centeredness. When we seek to get credit on this earth for the service we do, I suspect our efforts will not "count" in heaven. Mature spirituality challenges us to become a part of God's "secret service."

A Word of Caution

Indeed, it is possible to go through all the right motions of the disciplines, yet fail to accomplish their reason for being: the development of intimacy with God. The Pharisees were meticulous about observing the disciplines. However, they gave themselves to their observances for the purpose of being seen and receiving credit. Jesus recognized that, and even commented that they looked good on the outside, but were full of dead men's bones within. Their disciplines were *spiritual cosmetics*. They covered up their real selves with the niceness of good deeds and impressive adherence to carrying out the letter of the law.

Periodically, we need to do a reality check on our tendency to *do what we do to be seen and admired*. We must be real—not just go through the *motions* of spirituality like the

Pharisees. We must keep at the front of our minds and hearts the understanding that spiritual authenticity is a close relationship with the person of Christ—*not* an adherence to a set of "spiritual musts."

What Do the Disciplines Accomplish?

Why is each discipline a priority? To make our lives better? This happens, but this is not the basic intention. The deepest reason the disciplines are a priority in our lives is because we love God and we want to live our lives in ways that please Him and bring glory to Him. This happens only when we lovingly submit ourselves to His disciplines, His priorities, His concern for our fruitfulness.

What do the disciplines accomplish when we observe them authentically—not just move through the motions? They place us before God so that He can love us and minister to us, refine us, and gradually transform us into loving others while being witnesses and ministers to others. This is the process of growing deeper, of becoming, step by step, more like Christ. This is "the way" of Christ following—a pathway to Christlikeness.

"Spiritual discipline is the effort to create some space in which God can work."

—Henri Nouwen

"The best and most wonderful thing that can happen to you in this life, is that you should be silent and let God work."

—Dag Hammarskjöld

pathway five

MAKE PRAYER YOUR LIFE, AND YOUR LIFE, PRAYER

"[My determined purpose is] that I may know Him [that I may progressively become more deeply and intimately acquainted with Him, perceiving and recognizing and understanding the wonders of His Person more strongly and more clearly]."
—Philippians 3:10 AMP

rayer is as important to the soul of the Christ fol-lower as breathing is to the body. Prayer is the response language of the Christian walk. There is so much I want to say about prayer. How can I condense the supreme necessity of prayer into the few pages of one chapter?

Prayer—An Absolute Essential

Simply stated, prayer is essential in moving down each pathway discussed in this book. We cannot experience *any* of them adequately unless prayer becomes a natural, ever-present element flowing through our spiritual bloodstreams and saturating the far reaches of our lives. Christlikeness is impossible without authentic prayer. Without prayer, faith remains shallow and we do not experience the depths of God.

The Goal of Prayer. The goal of prayer is the goal of every aspect of the Christian life. It is best stated in the classic Westminster Shorter Catechism: "Man's chief end is to glorify God, and to enjoy Him for ever." Paul emphasized, "Whatever you do, do it all for the glory of God" (1 Corinthians 10:31). "Whatever" includes prayer.

The first part of this frequently quoted statement is often emphasized: "to glorify God." The latter part is not so often mentioned: "and to enjoy Him for ever." The psalmist exclaimed "Delight yourself in the LORD" (Psalm 37:4). Paul wrote, "Revel in him" (Philippians 4:4 *The Message*). Do you literally *enjoy* God in your praying? Enjoying Him is an important element in deepening our relationship with Him.

The Premise of Prayer. This premise is from my own "catechism": All the good, fine things we do for God are largely futile unless (1) they come from the mind of God (they are His idea, and not ours); (2) they are dedicated and offered to God and others in the spirit of Christ; and (3) they are carried out in the power and energy of the Holy Spirit, not our energy. This reminds us that the most important factor about prayer is not prayer. The most important aspect of prayer is God, His glory, and our current, close, costly relationship with Him. This, in turn, means that God does not just answer our *words*. He answers our *lives*.

This premise is fulfilled only when prayer
becomes the very essence of our beings.

The Two Purposes of Prayer. We must acknowledge the two
major purposes of prayer: (1) The first purpose is personal: to
know God in Christ intimately, to love Him increasingly, and
to become more and more like Him. Paul wrote, "Everything
else is worthless when compared with the priceless gain of
knowing Christ Jesus my Lord" (Philippians 3:8 NLT). Our
intimate walk with Him must be vital in order for our words to
be authentic prayer. The *walk* with Him and the *talk* with Him
are both crucial to Christlikeness. **Is knowing Christ your
passion?**

(2) The second major purpose of prayer is to partner with
Him, through prayer, in the doing of His Kingdom work in the
world. One of the most astounding Kingdom truths is that God
has chosen to accomplish His purposes in the world in response
to the prayers of His people. Does this mean He is powerless
without our prayers? Not at all! God can do anything He
desires, at any time, in any way He chooses. But He has made a
holy decision to give us this role of dynamic partnership with
Him. I have heard T. W. Hunt say time and again, "God refuses
to act alone." We do our part; God does His. Amazing!

The Meaning of Prayer. We may need to affirm our under-
standing of the real meaning of prayer. Prayer is, foundationally,
a love relationship with God. At the same time, prayer is a gauge
of our relationship with Him. Our prayer habits, attitudes, and
content reveal the state of the relationship.

Defining Prayer. Prayer is difficult to describe with mere
words, but let's try. Prayer has been referred to as either the

greatest thing we can know and do or the most cruel hoax possible. Prayer is, of course, communication with God—simple, honest, natural, conversational, personal. Prayer is talking to God as we talk to our best friend, because He *is* our best friend! Prayer is *embracing* Him with all our hearts. It is inviting Him into the very midst of our lives. Deep prayer is offering ourselves to Him every day, with no strings attached.

"Prayer is something even deeper than words. Prayer is an attitude of our hearts, an attitude of mind."

—O. Hallesby

"The essential act of prayer is not bending God's will to ours, but bending our will to His. Thus, our prayers should not be 'Please do for me what I want,' but 'Please do in me, with me, and through me what You want.'"

—Archbishop Temple

"Prayer is the central avenue God uses to transform us."

—Richard Foster

"Prayer is none other than an act of the believer working together with God."

—Watchman Nee

These views of prayer change our perspective and cause us to think God's thoughts after Him. We begin to pray what the Holy Spirit prompts us to pray. We begin, wonder of wonders, to have the mind of Christ. This is a vital pathway toward Christlikeness.

Is this happening to you?

God's Answers Come in Various Forms

Probably the most asked questions about prayer have to do with answers. As I was growing up, I was taught that God has three answers to our prayers: yes, no, and wait. Some say that one of God's answers is, "You've got to be kidding!" As I have become a bit more experienced in my own relationship with Him, I have discerned other answers. One is, "I will give you something even better than you asked!"

I love to hear dramatic stories of answered prayer. In my own journey, however, I rarely have dramatic experiences. The deepest answers to my prayers have not been measurable or tangible. My passionate belief is that God's greatest answer is the gift of Himself. Thomas à Kempis' prayer strikes a responsive chord in me:

"It is too small and unsatisfactory, whatever thou bestowest on me, apart from Thyself."

Likewise, Oswald Chambers' statement has special meaning to me:

"Spiritual lust makes me demand an answer from God, instead of seeking God who gives the answer....The meaning of prayer is that we get hold of God, not the answer."

When our Heavenly Father is the desire of our hearts (Isaiah 26:8), then *He* is our greatest answer.

Is He your greatest answer?

Make a Private Chapel of Your Heart

Making a private chapel of your heart means turning your being to the Father all through the day and night. It means "practicing the presence of God." Brother Lawrence wrote a classic book by that title. He said, "The time of business does not with me differ from the time of prayer; and in the noise and clatter of my kitchen, while several persons are at the same time calling for different things, I possess God in as great tranquility as if I were upon my knees in the chapel." Then he added, "Make a private chapel of your heart where you can retire from time to time to commune with Him."

I love those words. My own heart is moved every time they come to mind. This means the kitchen can be *our* private chapel, too. So can an office, a classroom, or a car—anytime, anywhere, we can be in our own private chapel. This is how we can pray without ceasing. This is how we can walk without fainting. This is how we "practice the presence of God"—at all times.

Prayer Brings Satan's Opposition

Even though Satan will ultimately be defeated, he is busy at work seeking to undermine and destroy the people of God and the work of God. Yet no one is a firmer believer in the power of prayer than Satan. Not that he practices it—he suffers from it. Satan must be gleeful when we fail to pray, for then we become vulnerable to his invasion of our attitudes and behavior.

"Be self-controlled and alert. Your enemy the devil prowls around like a roaring lion looking for someone to devour. Resist him, standing firm in the faith."

—1 Peter 5:8–9

Of course, Satan opposes prayer because prayer destroys him. Frankly, I am being plain dumb when I fail to take advantage of what God provides through prayer. Do you need to give yourself in a renewed way to the ultimate value of prayer in voiding the power of evil around you? I need and want this to take place within me and all around me.

Prayerlessness Is Sin

"As for me, far be it from me that I should sin against the LORD by failing to pray."

—1 Samuel 12:23

One of our greatest prayer concerns needs to be to pray that God's people will pray, for prayerlessness is sin. We may call it neglect or spiritual dryness, but God considers it sin.

At times we tend to believe that our greatest need in the area of prayer is training in prayer, or prayer materials, or retreats, or books on prayer. Although these matters are helpful to us, our greatest need is the inner power, strength, and stamina that comes from God Himself—His power stored in the inner recesses of our beings. Power for worship, witness, ministry, and mission. Power for living joyfully and abundantly, power to love, trust, and obey.

How do we access God's power, His spiritual energy and stamina? Only through prayer. God releases His Holy Spirit's transforming power in response to the prayers of His people. Pentecost came as the result of prayer—not preaching—but prayer; and prayer brought the Holy Spirit, who brought the power that transformed, clarified, and energized those first century disciples.

In studying the latter verses of the Gospels and the early part of Acts—those fifty days between Easter and Pentecost—

we find the disciples were tentative and uncertain about their own futures and the future of the floundering movement they were leading. They dearly loved the Lord, but they were quietly powerless. It was only after they rediscovered prayer that they became joyful, fruitful, consistent, radiant, full-of-power witnesses who turned the world upside down for Christ.

We, too, can get stuck in that same state in which those disciples found themselves. Some of us, perhaps many of us, in varying degrees, are powerless, fruitless, even shallow. Our priorities get hazy.

How can we have a rediscovery of power, of spiritual energy and stamina? The answer is the same for us as it was for them. We need a revival of prayer. Prayer leads to the Holy Spirit's filling, which leads to effective living and dying and to a portion of all the Christ-like qualities.

Will God do within us and among us what He did in their midst? How He wants to! But we must meet the conditions of prayer and open ourselves to the Holy Spirit's filling. We must have a revival of prayer in our deepest beings. This is imperative on our pathway journey toward Christlikeness.

Do we dare? Do you feel inadequate as you view your present life of prayer? It is never too late to "begin again" with God. In fact, He longs for your new beginning with Him.

"Nothing is ever wasted in the kingdom of God. Not one tear, not all our pain, not the unanswered prayers...nothing will be wasted if we give our lives to God. And if we are willing to be patient until the grace of God is made manifest, whether it takes one year or ninety, it will be worth the wait."

—Rebecca Manley Pippert

pathway six

PARTICIPATE FULLY IN YOUR CHURCH

"Let us consider how we may spur one another on toward love and good deeds. Let us not give up meeting together, as some are in the habit of doing, but let us encourage one another."

—Hebrews 10:24–25

"How wonderful it is, how pleasant, for God's people to live together in harmony!"

—Psalm 133:1 TEV

"You can develop a healthy, robust community that lives right with God and enjoy its results only if you do the hard work of getting along with each other, treating each other with dignity and honor."

—James 3:18 *The Message*

*F*or Christ followers with a strong commitment to take Jesus' teachings seriously, His church is a significant reality in their lives. Ideally, Christ following places His people in authentic community and fellowship with other believers. When their spirituality is for real, the "Christ in them" draws them to one another.

It happened that way from the very beginning of Jesus' ministry. He invited Simon and Andrew to leave their fishing nets and join Him in His mission on earth. Soon James and John responded to His invitation and became a part of a small but growing group. The shared fellowship Jesus and the disciples experienced would become characteristic of the infant New Testament congregations.

Later, John wrote, "It is what we have seen and heard that we are announcing to you, in order that you also may have partnership with us; and our partnership is with the Father and with his Son, Jesus Christ" (1 John 1:3 Phillips).

The New International Version translates this Scripture, "We proclaim to you what we have seen and heard, so that you also may have fellowship with us. And our fellowship is with the Father and with his Son, Jesus Christ."

Their interdependence was obvious. The phrase "one another" appears many times throughout the Scriptures. Even as the early disciples were Christ followers in the framework of a close community, we 21st century disciples are to nurture one another as His followers, His apprentices in this same expression of community.

Koinonia

The local congregation is God's biblical provision for relationships between Christians—relationships that result in our knowing one another and helping each other know Him.

Koinonia is the Greek word that has become well known as meaning "extraordinary fellowship." The term represents not a casual gathering but a deeply meaningful sharing of lives. Paul referred to the parts of the human body to make this point: "If one part suffers, every part suffers with it; if one part is honored, every part rejoices with it" (1 Corinthians 12:26). This closeness of fellowship is certainly God's intention for His people.

The Church at Its Best

This ideal is not always fulfilled. In fact, the word *church* triggers a wide variety of images. With over 2000 years of history, the impressions conjured up by the word *church* represent an entire range of emotions. Speak of church, and some people picture a "little brown church in the wildwood" attended by their grandparents, while others see in their mind's eye a very different scenario—a large cathedral with stained-glass windows.

For some, it is a building to which they were required to go without having a choice, and the impression lingers that church is something to be endured. Others think of church largely as a location where weddings and funerals take place. Then there are those who insist that church is a place of warmth and ever-new experiences with the living, reigning Lord and His people.

At its best, the church is a coming together of Christ followers who are moving alongside one another on an exciting, ever-unfolding spiritual journey. A faithful church offers regular opportunities for involvement in worship of the triune God, proclamation of the great good news of Jesus, opportunities for spiritual growth into Christlikeness, intentional ministries to those in need, and reaching out to others with the Good News, both locally and worldwide. The church at its best represents love for God and others and a desire to bring glory to Him.

A Place to Belong. Also at its best, the church is an extended family. Indeed, members belong to one another as well as to the Father of the family. I know of many examples of church members being closer to one another than they are to their own blood brothers and sisters. The healthy church family teaches and encourages us to care for one another as a natural result of the bonds binding our hearts together.

A Place to Become. Just as one's blood family provides many opportunities to learn and put into practice life's basic lessons, the Christ-centered church family provides ways and means for meeting the deep spiritual needs that encourage us on the pathway to Christlikeness. The church needs to provide a welcoming place for the seeker, the immature believer, the seasoned Christ follower, and also for those who have just "been around" for many years. We all need to come "Just as I am" with realistic expectations of helpful opportunities to become more and more the persons God had in mind when He made us. Regardless of how long we have been "in the family," we all desperately need to become more than we are. And we need help in doing so. Ideally, the church provides the appropriate care toward individual and corporate growth as the Body of Christ.

We are keenly aware that a significant component in this pathway is the role of the pastor. There is no way to emphasize enough the importance of the pastor in the life and leadership of the church. Suffice it to say that the Christ-following pastor, committed to Christ and to being like Him, loves and shepherds his congregation as he leads the church in the "ways of the Lord." His relationship with God is personal, strong, real, and transparent. His faith is vibrant and healthy. The church with this kind of pastor is blessed beyond measure.

A Place to Love and Be Loved. This is the acid test. Christlike love must be obvious and vital in His church. A congregation must reach out and connect with one another in tender ways. God will be pleased with a community that lives by the example Jesus set for us as the church becomes salt and light in a confused and confusing world.

"Love grows here."
—Sign on a church's billboard

At its best, the church can be a little picture of heaven on earth.

I have belonged to a wide variety of churches (simply because I have lived so long!). To a decided degree, I have been more than blessed by "my" churches. Yet, like many of you, I have seen firsthand the glaring imperfections of churches, for I am a part of the imperfections. I confess I have felt grief and disappointment at times because of how far a church can "miss the mark." Becoming like Christ is to do my part in helping my church to become as Christlike as it can become.

God's Plan for His People

God's plan for His church is to be a community of disciples who take seriously His Word—believing it, studying it, respecting it, absorbing it, understanding it, applying it to individual and community life, as well as developing a concerned, loving view of the lost world. The Father has so many things He wants to do in our world, and His stated plan is to use His people to accomplish His purposes. He wants to do this through His church.

We Christ followers are on this journey together, with the same desperate needs for receiving love and giving love to one another and to others—within the church and outside the congregation's framework. As *we* embrace the love Christ freely and abundantly gives to us, and also the love that comes from other Christ followers, then *we* have the capacity to pass this love on to others. As we receive affirmation, we have affirmation to give to others. As we are encouraged, God uses us to encourage others. As we grow toward Christlikeness, God empowers us to reveal His love to those around us.

Literally, God's plan is that we pass on to others what we have received. *Church* was designed in God's heart to provide generously what we, His people, need in order to become a part of the flow of His loving provision for others. Oh, the beauty and joy of being useful in the expression of God's love and care for His people! This is an intrinsic part of Christlikeness.

God is using many churches today in impressive ways to reach out in love to those within His church and to those outside the framework of His church. He is calling us to be *family* and *home on earth,* a little taste of heaven to one another and to those who do not know Him. Many churches are reaching out to places and peoples around the world, bearing witness of His redeeming love. Thousands of laypersons are going overseas on mission assignments, representing their Lord and their congregations as they serve alongside career missionaries in many meaningful ways. This is today's church truly being a New Testament congregation.

So join the church! I mean, really become an integral part of the Body of Christ of which you are a member. Don't stay on the fringe. Give yourself to Him and His Body whole-heartedly. For the Christ follower, the giving of oneself comes naturally.

An African Proverb

"A person becomes a person through other people. There can be no 'I' without you."

Even though this proverb is not from Scripture, it conveys a message that harmonizes with the Scriptures I have used in this discussion. Growing in Christlikeness requires other believers, a spiritual community of persons who want God to nourish their souls, as well as yours.

"We don't just *go* to church; we *are* the church."

—Ernest Southcott

"When we bring people to believe differently, they really do become different. One of the greatest weaknesses in our teaching and leadership today is that we spend so much time trying to get people to do things good people are supposed to do, without changing what they really believe. It doesn't succeed very well, and that is the open secret of church life."

—Dallas Willard

"The long experience of the church is more likely to lead to correct answers than the experience of the lone individual."

—Elton Trueblood

pathway seven

CULTIVATE MEANINGFUL RELATIONSHIPS

"What I mean is that both you and I will be helped at the same time, you by my faith and I by yours."

—Romans 1:12 TEV

"This love I speak of means that we must live in obedience to God's commands. The command, as you have all heard from the beginning, is that you must all live in love."

—2 John 1:6 TEV

"Put your life on the line for your friends."

—John 15:13 *The Message*

*Cl*ll of life for every one of us involves relating to people all day long every day. This statement is one *everyone* has heard and said…a real truism…so why take time and space to expound on it? The answer lies in the fact that too many of us are not very adept at relating to people. Therefore, we need to "get good" at it! Living in harmony with biblical relational principles is a high priority for the Christ follower.

We Need Closeness with People

Our Heavenly Father created us with a need for closeness with other human beings. Indeed, deep within us is an unquenchable hunger for soul mates and soul friends. Near the top of any list of "things that matter most" is a desire for healthy, meaningful relationships with the people who occupy our lives.

God, in His wisdom, did not only create the need, but He designed the plan to meet this need: family and friends. Over a lifetime, many different people have a major role in our spiritual and emotional health and growth. God-honoring relationships have the inherent and powerful potential for meeting our need for human love, affection, acceptance, trust, understanding, self-disclosure, and joy. Additionally, and very significantly, close relationships have the power to point us toward God—or away from Him.

Yet studies show that a high percentage of Americans suffer from loneliness and from feeling deprived of the closeness for which every human being longs. A comedian jokes, and it hits a responsive chord, "Remember, we are all in this—alone!"

Vernon Grounds writes in *Establishing a Faith Fellowship*, "We were made to enter into a relationship of love and trust and service with other people. And unless we do this, we become emotionally sick, miserable, and frustrated." We must give our attention to this strong warning.

Broken Relationships

All around us, and within our own families, we see and experience broken relationships. Death takes its toll in separating those who love one another. Divorce is rampant with unparalleled numbers of marriages breaking apart. Someone said that multiple divorces make family trees look like they have been hit by lightning.

Many children grow up in complex home situations without living with both their biological parents. Of course, this creates additional fragmentation and complexities. Disappointment, betrayal, distance, and hurts lash out with various intensities, undermining and destroying relationships that had been cherished at an earlier time. Still, God created us with the intention and capacity to meet our relational human needs in one another.

This means that the deepest lessons related to life and faith are not learned in isolation. They are learned with and from family members, close friends, coworkers, neighbors, authors, and even casual acquaintances whose paths we cross without intention, but whose influence sinks into our souls and lodges there.

Obviously, the path to meaningful relationships is not an easy path, for we must submit ourselves to the difficult task of accepting, understanding, loving, and caring for one another. Yet even in the midst of all the problems that invariably come from our being connected to others, there is no adequate substitute for the potential richness of close relationships.

The Most Important Family Relationship

The one family relationship more important than our earthly family is our place in the family of God.

"He has given us the privilege of being born again, so that we are now members of God's own family."
—1 Peter 1:3 TLB

Relationship with the God of the universe is the ultimate foundation of life itself—knowing Him intimately as our heavenly Father, loving Him supremely, and seeking to become more and more like Him. Being born into God's family places all His limitless resources at our disposal for growing up and growing deep. This new birth brings the unparalleled privilege of eternal life with Him, which has already begun for the Christ follower.

As important as it is, the home, of course, is not the only location for meaningful relationships. In fact, the church *can* step into those sad, blank places where the family has failed. Or perhaps there is no family, and there is a need for a meaningful alternative to the home that did not come through. The church, when it is fulfilling its mission, becomes the family of God. This is our Lord's intention. The church can be, at last, a most meaningful *home* for those who are spiritually homeless. The fact remains that God wants each of us to be a vital part of His family.

Thus, two of the essentials of Christ following are:
∼ We need to experience *human* love, trust, and joy.
∼ We need to experience *divine* love, trust, and joy.

The Matchless Joy of Cherishing Your Family

Let us focus special attention on the importance of your earthly family—and mine. Family is God's idea. To be nurtured and cared for within the framework of a family is His plan. If you do not have the matchless joy of a family that cherishes one another, take stock of what needs to be done to bring this priority into being.

Indeed, each of us is here because we belong to a family. Even so, we must admit the devastating truth that there are too many today who live within some form of family relationship, but without the warmth of family love and care.

Alienation within so many families, including Christian families, is alarming. As bonds have increasingly unraveled, the dysfunctional family has become more and more the norm. This reality has created a culture and a generation that is the product of dramatically changed moral and social values. Not only does this picture have serious consequences for the family, but for every aspect of our society. This dysfunctional condition is *not* God's plan.

God's plan is for family members to point one another to Himself, to model His love to one another, to our extended families, and to the world beyond our families. However, much too frequently, the family is broken, and God's plan falls apart. What can be done to fix it?

The answer is a spiritual one. I do not want to oversimplify, but we must go to our Heavenly Father, first of all, alone, confessing our own sin and neediness, and asking His forgiveness. None of us is completely pure in family living. Each of us has contributed our share of brokenness.

Then we must go to one another within the family circle and follow the same process of confession and asking forgiveness from one another. True confession is so freeing, and forgiveness is so sweet. Yes, this is very difficult to do, but so absolutely necessary.

Husbands and wives *can* become lovers again; brothers and sisters *can* become best friends. There is much to be learned from one another about inner wellness, and much to be passed on to those who follow us in the generational pattern. We need to get it right—now! If we fail at this level of relationship within the home and family, nothing can compensate for the breakdown.

A Lifestyle of Love and Trust

Love is such a familiar word. We say it so glibly and refer to a lifestyle of love almost abstractly. However, love must be translated into very practical, everyday terms as we relate to one another as families, coworkers, fellow church members, schoolmates, etc. Love and trust need to be "seen" and experienced in the ordinary transactions of daily life.

Realistically, how does this happen?

There is no new answer to this important question. We must open ourselves to the Father and offer ourselves as a vessel through which His love will flow freely into the lives of others. As we make ourselves available to Him in love, trust, and obedience, He is eager to make His home in us (amazing!), and allow His love to flow freely through us into the lives of others. Our challenge is to be a consistent channel of God's free-flowing resources into the lives of those to whom we relate.

I am inclined to being practical. I love workable ideas I can promptly put into action. Therefore, I want to share one of the most helpful relational measures I know. It comes from Stephen Covey's book, *The Seven Habits of Highly Successful People*. Many are already familiar with the concept. I have found the idea making a difference in my own relationships, and I enjoy passing it on to others.

Your Emotional Bank Account—and Mine

Dr. Covey writes about the concept of an "emotional bank account." This is a metaphor used to describe the amount of trust being gradually built into a relationship. It represents the sense of safety one has with another human being. We all have an emotional bank account. We are either making deposits to or withdrawals from one another's emotional bank accounts.

For example, I make a deposit in my account with you every time I treat you with courtesy, honesty, kindness, sensitivity—every time I keep a commitment to you, each time I give you a sincere affirmation, and so on. The result is that my account with you builds each time I make a deposit. Every deposit causes your trust of me to grow and expand. As I make more and more deposits, your trust of me becomes strong.

I can also "stump my toe" with you, meaning I make a mistake in relation to you, or create a misunderstanding, thus causing a withdrawal from the account. However, if there have been enough deposits and the trust level is high enough, then the emotional reserve will compensate. In other words, I have invested enough in my account with you previously so that our relationship can "take it" without your feelings getting ruffled and a rift developing.

Conversely, when I become angry with you, or insensitive, or discourteous, or betray a confidence, or fail to keep a commitment, or disappoint you, then a withdrawal from the account takes place. At some point, when enough withdrawals have taken place, the account becomes depleted. By that time, our relationship becomes troubled and unstable. One thing after another "goes wrong" as we interact. Eventually, the relationship may fall apart.

My Emotional Bank Account Withdrawal

Several years ago, I initiated a plan with some dear friends (a deposit) to meet me for a special time together. After discussing several possibilities, we agreed on a date and time. I failed to write the occasion on my calendar and had planted in my feeble mind another of the dates we discussed—a later date than the one we had actually set. Of course, when that day came, I did not show up (a withdrawal).

When they called to find out what happened and I realized my mistake, I felt terribly embarrassed and chagrined, of course. For a second or two, I wanted to "eat worms." However, we have a long history of love deposits in one another's emotional bank accounts, and there was plenty of trust and love built up. Therefore, my friends were genuinely gracious and understanding. There was no love lost.

When the trust account is high, communication is easy and free flowing. A mistake is no big deal. But if I have a history with you of being thoughtless or discourteous, or if I have betrayed a confidence, or disappointed you, eventually the account gets overdrawn. Along the way, we would have begun to measure our words and walk on eggshells with one another. Perhaps, eventually, we would even allow the friendship to dissolve.

*D*oes this ring any bells with anyone out there?

We find this principle quietly, and sometimes noisily, at work in our families. Many marriages fail to develop intimacy and deep understanding because of this breakdown—this lack of deposits in each other.

Also, this principle of the emotional bank accounts is very much at work in our churches. We have unresolved disagreements, and we withdraw from one another or become defensive. People leave churches over such situations. In churches where there is much bonding, unity, and service to and alongside one another, emotional bank accounts receive many deposits. Relationships are secure and free flowing because of ample deposits in both directions.

One word of warning: the closer the relationship, the more regularly deposits need to be made. In every healthy, vital connection, continual deposits are taking take place.

Deposits that Build Up Emotional Bank Accounts

Practical person that I am, I appreciate specifics in terms of suggestions for "deposits." Covey names some everyday relational measures that invariably build up accounts—simple things we can all do. They are:

∾ Understanding the individual. (It is so wonderful to be understood!) People like people who genuinely are seeking to understand them. Often, folks are not listening to understand, but only politely waiting to reply.

∾ Giving attention to little things. (The little things are the big things.)

∾ Keeping your commitments. (A promise is a major deposit; a broken promise is a major withdrawal.)

∾ Making expectations clear. (Goals and roles must be on the table or else conflicting expectations will easily arise.)

∾ Showing personal integrity. (Truth-telling, keeping promises, treating everyone by the same set of principles, conforming our words to reality.)

∾ Apologizing sincerely when you make a withdrawal. (Weak people cannot apologize. Sincerely saying "I was wrong" makes a huge deposit.)

Look within your relationships and examine them by the above six measures. Which of your relationships are near bankruptcy? What can you do to make a genuine deposit into another's emotional bank account? Remember, the deposit must be real!

A crucial relational principle I want to drop into this mix is this:

*T*ake yourself out of the center of the universe.

"Give away your life; you'll find life given back, but not merely given back—given back with bonus and blessing. Giving, not getting, is the way. Generosity begets generosity."
—Luke 6:38 *The Message*

Jesus spoke a crucial truth to which we must give serious attention. Our human tendency (to put it mildly) is to place ourselves in the center of our universe, and in subtle ways we let it be known that people and situations must revolve around our preferences and needs. When we do so, we are *not* following Christ. We are following our own self-centered tendencies.

"If anyone would come after me, he must deny himself and take up his cross daily and follow me."
—Luke 9:23

I affirm the importance of knowing ourselves, accepting ourselves from God's perspective, and recognizing our value as the Father's children, whom He loves with a perfect love. Indeed, I have observed the factor of self-esteem for many years. I think I understand its basic importance and its need to deepen and grow within each of us.

Also, unless we have resolved the hurts and wounds in our past and come to terms with our basic value in our souls, we will be slapped around by waves of insecurities and fears, and we will forever interpret situations in terms of how they affect *us*. We will "set up camp" in the center of our own personal universe.

Our feelings will be easily ruffled. We will take interactions with others negatively and personally when they were not intended that way. We will have unrealistic expectations of people and then be frequently disappointed by them. We will have a need to be right, an inward striving to get recognition, to subtly exalt ourselves, and protect ourselves. We will do everything we do, ultimately, for ourselves. (Hear any bells ringing?)

What a heavy baggage it is to live this way! It is so freeing to come to the place where we can take ourselves out of the center of the universe through simple surrender—and place God there. This act removes a huge inward burden. We can then say—and mean—those profound, but difficult words: "I was wrong. Please forgive me."

Such words magically transform the atmosphere of a relationship, a family, a committee, a church. It is wonderfully liberating when we are freed from dwelling on our ego's nagging whimpers and our self-image's sagging negativity. We must take ourselves out of the center of the universe...and place God there! Only the grace and work of the Holy Spirit can bring about this magnificent exchange. Every morning, before I move a muscle, I ask Him to make this exchange for me.

Frankly, I wish everyone you live with could grasp and practice this spiritual principle. I realize some of you live with someone (or perhaps more than one) who has moved squarely into the center of his or her universe. They expect you to respect their location, and they want *you* to revolve around *them*. Each of us can follow this spiritual dimension only for ourselves. Jesus said:

"Give away your life; you'll find life given back, but not merely given back—given back with bonus and blessing."

—Luke 6:38

Many of our families and our churches need a revival of relationship. We would do well to give special attention, biblically and relationally, to the quality of our ability to relate, lovingly and authentically, to one another. The way we interface with one another gives a clue as to the quality of our relationship with Christ, as well as to the depths of our relationship with God.

"Very few people are without deep negative feelings toward others who are or have been closely related to them. Wounds carried steadily through the years have weighted us down and prevented spiritual growth in love, joy, and peace. They may have seeped over into our identity. We wouldn't know who we are without them. But they can be healed or dismissed, if we are ready to give them up to God and receive the healing ministry of His Word and spirit."

—Dallas Willard

pathway eight

SERVE THE LORD AND OTHERS— WITH GLADNESS

"Your attitude must be like my own, for I, the Messiah, did not come to be served, but to serve and to give my life."
—Matthew 20:28 TLB

God created us and gifted us to make a difference on planet earth for Him and His Kingdom. To fulfill His plan, we are to pattern our lives after the example of Jesus, who did not come to be served, but to serve and to give His life. This sums up the magnificent mission of our Lord. For those of us who seek to be His followers, His mission is also the bottom line of *our* reason for being. Service is not optional for Christ followers.

"It is he who saved us and chose us for his holy work, not because we deserved it, but because that was his plan."

—2 Timothy 1:9 TLB

"It is God himself who has made us what we are and given us new lives from Christ Jesus, and long ago he planned that we should spend these lives in helping others."

—Ephesians 2:10 TLB

The Scriptures almost overwhelm us with assurances that God made us and saved us for the purpose of serving Him by helping others. From the beginning, He had this in His plan for us—service and ministry in His church and His Kingdom—a special assignment for every one of us to fulfill. Accepting and fulfilling His personal design and calling was never intended to be optional.

You may be thinking, "But I am a layperson. I'm not *called*." However, Paul was not writing to a group of ministers. He was writing to the congregation at Ephesus. He insisted that the Father calls *every* member of the Body to a specific assignment designed to enhance His Kingdom.

God's Call—A Prominent Biblical Concept

Call is a term used in some form over 700 times in Scripture. Just that statistic reveals a compelling biblical theme. The word is used to describe God's close involvements with His people, individually and corporately.

Corporately, God called Israel to be His people. One by one, He called Moses, Samuel, Gideon, David, Jeremiah,

Esther, Deborah, John the Baptist, the disciples, Paul, Aquila and Priscilla, Lydia, Phoebe, and of course, many others. Consider also His call to Martin Luther, Jonathan Edwards, John Wesley, William Carey, Ann and Adoniram Judson, Mother Teresa, Lottie Moon, and you and me.

God's call to each of them, and to each of us, is among other things a special gift, the pearl of great price, the treasure in the field. His call is written into the fabric of the Christ follower's soul. Consider briefly a simplified outline of God's calls to Christ followers:

1. God calls each of us into His Kingdom. He calls us to salvation, to be His disciples, to love our neighbors, to obey and trust Him, and to bear witness of His Son.

2. He calls us to do the daily tasks before us that include our roles and relationships in everyday life. For example, the Father calls us to relate lovingly to our families every day. In every task, duty, responsibility—all the matters that are an integral part of everyday life—God calls us to fulfill them with love and grace, as the "Christ in us" must do. This is the real significance of Christlikeness.

3. The third calling relates to an understanding of one's profession or job. Some persons feel a strong call to be a doctor, teacher, engineer, or one of the many forms of vocational secular work. We must acknowledge that God calls every Christ follower into full-time Christian ministry, regardless of one's work or profession. Every Christ follower is on call at all times, including through one's work, to be a witness, a disciple, and a doer of the Word. Indeed, God calls His people into secular positions to be Kingdom people in the marketplace.

Martin Luther and other reformers proclaimed the significance of *every* Christian's responsibility and accountability to God. Luther declared *all* work as sacred, if offered as to the Lord. The holy people were not only those cloistered in the monasteries and convents. Luther said the milkmaid could milk cows for the glory of God! Laity were then and are today called of God to have a significant role in His kingdom.

4. God calls some uniquely into vocational ministry, and He adequately equips those whom He calls for this work. Those who respond to this specific call relate directly to the "equipping of the laity." God calls them to prepare, assist, motivate, and encourage Christ followers to *live* as Christ followers, and to obediently fulfill the work of His Kingdom. This call involves the unique purpose or mission the Father has written deep within the Christ follower's soul.

God's Call Is to Serve with Gladness

We may be tempted to believe that God's call and plan for us is difficult to discern. I do not want to oversimplify this significant and sensitive part of our relationship with Him. However, the simple truth is that He has a call and a plan for each of us. We are called to serve Him. But then, this is not the whole of His intention. We are not only to serve Him, but to do so with gladness. "Serve the LORD with gladness" (Psalm 100:2 AMP).

The Bible makes it clear in many places that we are not to offer our service to Him grudgingly, but joyfully. Realistically, however, there are times when we are pressed into service, when there is a ministry to be done, and no one else to do it. I call it "drudgery service." How can we serve the Lord "with gladness" under these circumstances? Words from an Old Testament leader are helpful to me.

"But be sure to fear the LORD and serve him faithfully with all your heart; consider what great things he has done for you."
—1 Samuel 12:24

Our service for the Lord *can* create a gladness of spirit when we take into consideration the great things He has done for us. In fact, we discover we owe Him our very lives—a transforming reminder for the earnest Christ follower. Do you often meditate upon all the Lord has done for you?

Consider again the simplicity and priority of our mission to "serve the Lord with gladness." The psalmist certainly felt spontaneously glad. He exclaimed, "How can I repay the LORD for all His goodness to me?" (Psalm 116:12).

Service to others is one way of quietly, consistently saying "thank you" to Him and bringing glory to His holy name. In focusing on all He has done for us, we realize we can never serve Him enough, or thank Him enough for the privilege of service.

If we serve for any other reason than doing it "as to the Lord" in gratitude and thanksgiving for all He has done for us, then there may develop a mixed sense of drudgery in our service. To put it mildly, this is *not* the way God wants us to offer our service to Him.

We come back to our reason for being: to spend our lives in helping others—serving the Lord and others with gladness. We must not sit on the spiritual sidelines as a spectator, watching others do the work of service in the Kingdom. It is a matter of obedience. In fact, *not* to serve the Lord is a sin.

Our Example of Jesus as Servant

"Your attitude should be the same as that of Christ Jesus: Who, being in very nature God…made himself nothing, taking the very nature of a servant."

—Philippians 2:5–7

Jesus "did not come to be served, but to serve" (Mark 10:45). He gave himself generously and tenderly, ministering to the physical and spiritual needs of people. He focused His attention on the outcasts of society—tax collectors, beggars, lepers, and "unclean" women.

Jesus was the consummate servant. He was astonishingly humble as He washed the feet of His disciples, being an example for all His followers through all the ages to come. However, the ultimate act of servanthood and sacrifice was His crucifixion in our stead, fulfilling the words of the prophet Isaiah:

"Surely he took up our infirmities and carried our sorrows, yet we considered him stricken by God, smitten by him, and afflicted. But he was pierced for our transgressions, he was crushed for our iniquities; the punishment that brought us peace was upon him, and by his wounds we are healed."

—Isaiah 53:4–5

Our own hearts are moved as we pause and meditate on what His servant heart led Him to do in taking upon Himself the punishment that we ourselves deserve.

Not only does God have a calling for each of us to fulfill, but He has in mind a specific area of service for every one of His children. Regardless of what our vocation might be, He calls each of us—*every* follower of Christ—to specific service.

Spiritual Gifts—Another Key to Obedient Service

God has molded us so that we have exactly what we need to effectively accomplish what He has in mind for us to do. He has given us the abilities, talents, gifts, interests, and personalities to fulfill both His calling and His plan for service. These *special* abilities He has bestowed on us are *spiritual* gifts. Paul discusses this strategic subject in 1 Corinthians 12.

114

Consider several of the major points of his letter to the church in Corinth and to us:

"A spiritual gift is given to each of us as a means of helping the entire church."

—1 Corinthians 12:7 NLT

"It is the one and only Holy Spirit who distributes these gifts. He alone decides which gift each person should have."

—1 Corinthians 12:11 NLT

Let's be very practical. How can we discern what our spiritual gifts are? To consider this significant area of the Christ-following life, answer these personal questions:

≈ What are your deep-down interests? What captures your attention? What moves you?

≈ What do you *love* to do? What do you do well? Where can you serve that will fit who you are in your heart and soul?

≈ Do you listen attentively to the quiet, still voice of God? Are you aware of his soft and sometimes firm nudges toward certain aspects of service?

≈ Are you willing to try a type of service you have not considered before?

≈ Are you willing to "dive in" and work in a place of need and experiment to see if you are indeed gifted for that type of service?

Another Bottom Line
"Freely you have received, freely give."

—Matthew 10:8

The bottom line of this discussion is: we have been given much. Very likely, we have abilities that we do not realize we have because we have never agreed to exercise them. God knows us inside and out. We can have complete confidence that He will never lead us to do anything He has not given us the ability to do. He is too wise to do otherwise. We can trust Him to "take advantage" of the totality of our abilities, talents, temperament, inclinations, and life experiences and use them to do His work. We can be confident He will not waste any aspect of what we offer to do for His glory. Out of gratitude, humility, and love of God and others, we must pass it on.

**Are you willing and ready to allow
serving God and others to be a natural,
constant flow of your daily life?**

What Does It Mean to Be a Servant?

We come back to the place we began. We know that Christian servants serve and give because that's what Jesus did when He was on earth. Servants make themselves available at all times, even as He did then, and does today. Servants respond to whatever needs to be done on the spot as well as over the long haul. They give to others whatever they have to give, without waiting to be perfectly prepared.

Servants think about others rather than their own interests. They have genuine humility. They think of serving as a privilege, not an obligation they are fulfilling.

Real servants have authentic humility. Nothing is beneath their dignity to do. Whatever service they do, they do with all their hearts. Recently, my daughter quoted her pastor as saying, "God does not call the qualified; He qualifies the called."

Accounting Day Someday

Someday "each of us will have to give a personal account to God" (Romans 14:12 NLT) for our servanthood, or lack of it. What if the accounting we must give will include a report on how much time and attention we gave to ourselves, and how much time and energy we spent on others? What a sobering thought! At least, it is for me.

I recall a chorus we sang in my childhood and youth:

"Others, Lord, yes, others.
May this my motto be
Help me to live for others
That I may live for thee."

When our younger daughter, Debra, was in her early teens, one of her assigned church missions group activities was to have a service project for several months. She investigated some possibilities, and chose one to which she felt drawn. She committed herself to go to a nursing home weekly to visit a specific lady who had no living relatives. Mrs. Anderson was bedridden and immobilized by her aged condition.

Of course, I was the driver who took Deb for her weekly visits. Immediately, we both fell in love with Mrs. Anderson, a pretty, quiet, sweet little woman in her 90s who looked like an elderly angel. To our further delight, Mrs. Anderson had a spunky, mischievous roommate, Mrs. Messick, who did not have Mrs. Anderson's beauty, but made us laugh much of the time we were with them.

We found ourselves especially looking forward to these weekly visits. The three- month period passed quickly. When we completed the required assignment, we gave no thought to discontinuing our visits. We were hooked! The time came when we mourned the death of Mrs. Anderson. However, we had fully adopted Mrs. Messick also. We continued to make the weekly visits, with our love and attachment for our elderly friend continuing to deepen. Several years later, shortly before Debra left for college, Mrs. Messick died, bringing to an earthly end a friendship that had been one of the most meaningful experiences we had shared together in Deb's teenage years.

Now, these many years later, Deb and I still mention those two dear friends who had started out as a service "project." Even though this began as a matter of serving and ministering to others, we have acknowledged to one another many times that we were the ones most blessed.

Now, today, Debbie is taking her daughter, Emily, aged 14, to a nursing home regularly to visit with a certain "adopted" elderly friend, and they are repeating the scene I just described from 30 years ago. What God leads us to do in terms of service does not always turn out so delightfully as this one, but He smiles on our attempts to serve Him by serving others. In fact, He gives us major portions of satisfaction and joy.

I recall my older daughter, Meme, having an unusual experience of service as a teenager. Our church, located near downtown in a high crime area (at that time), sponsored a full-scale weekday ministries program for the families who lived in the neighborhood. We had ministries for all ages, and provided many special activities throughout the week.

Meme, in her high school and college years, was a professional model in her spare time. While in high school, periodically, she would lead a series of modeling classes for the neighborhood teenage girls as a part of their weekly evening class at our church. From time to time, I would slip in and watch Meme teaching the girls how, for example, to walk gracefully, how to sit properly, appropriate table manners, etc. I went to observe because I was fascinated to see the teenagers making changes from week to week before my eyes—socially, physically, and spiritually.

Now, today, Meme and her daughter, Lauren, are deeply involved in multiple service projects, depending on the season of the year. In the summertime, they go two weekday mornings every week (at 6:00 A.M.!) to participate in preparing and feeding breakfast to the homeless at their downtown church. They take with them a vanload of neighbors they have enlisted to help. Meme and her husband H.W. each serve as tutors working with an assigned ethnic child struggling with language competencies. Meme also has a regular assignment working with their church's lay visitation program in the local hospitals.

Serving God and others takes many forms. There are so many needs all around us we can meet. God is calling every solitary one of us into His service, in Jesus' name. The Bible makes it clear concerning God's expectation—that every Christ follower is called and expected to serve. Service is never an option.

Reflect upon these summary guidelines for service:

~ As much as is humanly possible, we are to discipline ourselves to serve God with our natural abilities. In that process, we are likely to discover our spiritual gift.

~ We must be willing to serve whether or not the service is exciting. We need to be willing to do the routine, less glamorous acts of service, and to do them with gladness.

~ We are called as long as we have health to "give ourselves away." On this earth, there is no "graduation" from serving the Lord.

∾ We are to serve like Jesus served, spontaneously meeting needs as we encounter them.

∾ God calls us to serve Him away from the spotlight—with no observers in sight. Personally, I am convinced it is good for me to do service no one knows about. In fact, it is *imperative*. Every Christ follower needs to be involved in some service that receives no recognition—at least on earth! We need to experience service for the sheer joy of giving ourselves to God and others with no strings attached.

∾ Serving others gives us a "spiritual workout." It stretches and enlarges our hearts. We need to serve, in some instances, even more than the "recipient" of our serving needs our ministry.

"We are God's workmanship, created in Christ Jesus to do good works, which God prepared in advance for us to do."
—Ephesians 2:10

What a powerful, sobering statement! This verse brings us back to the beginning of this pathway. God's call is clear and strong: we are to make a difference in this world—through service.

Are you right now engaged in a God-called service or ministry that is making a difference for Him and also for others?

pathway nine

DEEPLY RESPECT
THE LAW
OF THE HARVEST

"Don't be misled: No one makes a fool of God. What a person plants, he will harvest. The person who plants selfishness, ignoring the needs of others—ignoring God!—harvests a crop of weeds. But the one who plants in response to God, letting God's Spirit do the growth work in him, harvests a crop of real life, eternal life."
—Galatians 6:7–8 *The Message*

The law of the harvest is another ancient truth God has written into the fabric of the universe. The Bible and all the earth recommend we *choose* what we *want* to reap, and *then* plant the seeds that will produce whatever it is we desire to incorporate into our lives and relationships. In other words, when I want to grow tomatoes, I don't plant cucumbers. Duh!

Thus, down-to-earth common sense decrees we can choose what we harvest by wisely choosing what we sow. This basic truth applies just as faithfully to our lives. Even as I write these words, our country continues to reel from the financial devastation caused by business executives who did not consider the law of the harvest as they chose dishonest ways to doctor their books to show non-existent profits. Surely you remember the high-profile, now-bankrupt companies destroyed by their leaders' deceit. We can be sure our sins will find us out—if not in public at least in private, and if not in this life then certainly in the next.

So what do you want to harvest in your life? Since you cannot answer me directly, allow me to guess. Down deep, you want a life and a home saturated, not with a crop of emotional "weeds," but with love, affirmation, respect, harmony, joy, and serenity. You want meaningful work, health, energy, an effective vocation, a God-called, Christ-honoring ministry and/or service, and also very importantly, children and grandchildren who turn out all right. On a basic level, you want to go to bed at night feeling good about the day.

What would you add to your desired "crop?"

Good ideas? Surely. Realistic? Yes indeed, *if* you plant the seeds that will produce the fruit you want most to harvest in your life. Of course, fertilize the seeds you plant with prayer and time in God's Word. God will do His part. Nurture the gradual growth of your planted "seeds" with the Father's resources of love, peace, patience, goodness, gentleness, self control, and most of all, His limitless guidance and help.

Weeds Galore

I must be quick to acknowledge that other peoples' choices, some of them ungodly or the result of negligence, get factored into the equation of our own lives. Granted, when this happens, life becomes very complex. We cannot control the planting or harvesting of others, which leads to times and occasions when the consequences of their unwise choices spill over into our lives and our carefully-made plans.

Yes, weeds come up that we did not plant. Expect them. Weeds "show up" as a part of living life in our fallen world. The Evil One moves in at every point he can and creates "weeds." We must be alert to respond to Satan's ungodly moves in God-honoring ways. All of us are planting seeds each day that *will* come up.

When we deeply respect the law of the harvest and live in harmony with this reality, God promises us that stabilization will take place below the waterline. Since we will have carefully planted seeds that we consciously chose to plant, we can look forward to the godly harvest those seeds will bring. The Christ follower needs this spiritual dimension and confidence today and everyday.

As we have already acknowledged, some blame God for allowing negatives to happen in their lives. However, this law is a part of the order of the universe in which we live. The principle is a necessary one. We only control what *we* plant, and our own planting comprises a large and supremely important part of what happens in our lives. To live meaningfully in our universe, we must recognize the reliability of the law of the harvest, and live in harmony with it.

"What a person plants, he will harvest." The truth of the law of the harvest stands tall. When we choose our behavior, we are simultaneously choosing (in large part) the consequences. Our challenge is to plant carefully and wisely, in harmony with God's ways and His guidance, with ultimate respect for the way He has created us, called us, and designed us to live.

Therefore, let us be patient and consistent, in every season, to plant what we truly desire to reap: in our families, our work, our churches, and our lives. Observing the law of the harvest is another crucial pathway to Christlike spirituality.

"The greatest challenge here is faithfulness, which must be lived in the choices of every moment. When your eating, drinking, working, playing, speaking, or writing is no longer for the glory of God, you should stop it immediately, because you no longer live for the glory of God, you begin living for your own glory. Then you will separate yourself from God and do yourself harm."

—Henri Nouwen

"The world is filled with willing people; some willing to work, the rest willing to let them."

—Robert Frost

pathway ten

Do Your Best Living in the Present Tense

"Lord, remind me how brief my time on earth will be. Remind me that my days are numbered, and that my life is fleeting away."
—Psalm 39:4 NLT

"Whatever your hand finds to do, do it with all your might, for in the grave, where you are going, there is neither working nor planning nor knowledge nor wisdom."
—Ecclesiastes 9:10

*F*or many years, I have slowly opened my sleepy eyes to take in two framed messages on small easels on my bedside table. One contains words from a psalm, and the other a Sanskrit proverb. The verse is a familiar one:

"This is the day the LORD has made; let us rejoice and be glad in it."
—Psalm 118:24

The Message paraphrases the second part of this verse: "Let's celebrate and be festive!" Morning person that I am not, Eugene Peterson's interpretation (*The Message*) of the psalmist's words are a little too energetic for me the first thing in the morning. I do switch over to them later in the day. However, in those very early moments, I stay with the more laid-back NIV!

I do take the psalmist's words seriously. They help me set the tone for each day, and have done so for many years. I allow the words to remind me again (actually, before I have even moved a muscle) that this very day is a unique, unrepeatable gift. The Father is faithful to implant within me again the timeless principle: If I don't live vitally and wholeheartedly *this* day, in the midst of *whatever* the circumstances, I will squander an irreplaceable set of moments. My commitment is to keep this truth at the front of my heart, for I know I am capable of being distracted from living the next sixteen hours aware of the intense value of *this* day, these present moments. Indeed, God is offering *today* to each one of us as another opportunity to embrace and savor life.

Putting Off Our Best Living

At the same time, we can easily be distracted from this truth and find ourselves putting off our "real" and "best" living until some later time, until some current complexity solves or dissolves itself. Of course, we intend to focus on those matters essential to the soul and to life in the Kingdom—later. *Now* can get lost in the shuffle of the nagging details of today's busyness and hassle.

Periodically we read or hear someone challenging us to do our best living today—*this day, now, in the current moment*—giving our best focus and energy to becoming more like Christ and bringing glory to God. We may not respond aloud, but we might be saying under our breath, "Look, if only you knew all I am dealing with right now—in my marriage, my family, my work, my church, my relationships, my problems—you would understand why I cannot make this kind of commitment to live *this* day in an extraordinary way."

"Later, another day," we may say to ourselves, "when 'things' clear up and/or improve, I will, at *that* time, come to the place of doing my best living. But don't tell me to do it *now*—for I have all these counterproductive matters clouding, or even pouring rain, into my life."

The sad truth is that when we wait for some future time to do our best living, that perfect future time has a way of never showing up. "Another day, I will do my best living," we keep indicating by our actions or words, "but not today." Too often, that day never arrives for the person who puts off the resolve to do one's best living now—*this* day.

Look to *This* Day

Back to my bedside table. The other lines that greet me when I open my eyes to the light of day remind me repeatedly of the same valuable lesson:

Look to *this* day
For yesterday is only a dream
And tomorrow is only a vision.
But *today*, *well lived*
Makes every yesterday a dream of happiness
And every tomorrow a vision of hope.
Look well, therefore, to this day.

—Sanskrit Proverb

Today, Well Lived

Today, well lived...this is God's call to every Christ follower—to live *this* day well. I need this reminder from Him every morning of my life, and I keep the words prominently before me, just in case....

We would do well to join John Henry Jowett in the prayer he prayed in his book, *Yet Another Day*: "My Father, give me a sense of the unspeakable value of time. May I so live as to place a jewel in every moment."

In other words that are old and worn, yet very true: "Live your life each day as though this is the last day of your life. One day, it will be." When we do our best intentional living *this* day, with God's help, *now*, quiet contentment and deep satisfaction flow through us, and into the lives of others!

As always, in all things, Jesus is our model. He lived each day well, doing whatever needed to be done in the present tense. When He needed time alone with the Father, He gave that need priority. When He needed to be involved with people, He gave Himself to that agenda. He took time to select the appropriate action for the current moment, in the *now*. The Father always gave Him close guidance. He will do the same for each of us as well.

128

Living Each Day So There Will Be No Regret

Thus, a bottom-line, consecrated common sense conviction is: Live each day well, so that, as much as possible, you will have no regret. Stop, think, and ask yourself: Will I someday look back to this day with sadness, wishing I could live today over again in order to choose a different action, a better decision, some other attitude…or will I look back in gratitude for having sought and followed God's discernment and direction with the desire to do the right thing in the right way?

Compared to the history of the universe—and what about compared to eternity?—we are on planet earth for such a miniscule number of days. How significant it is to live these comparatively few days in the fullest, most meaningful way.

"Friends, this world is not your home, so don't make yourselves cozy in it. Don't indulge your ego at the expense of your soul."
—1 Peter 2:11 *The Message*

In the brief time we are on this earth, we are challenged again and again to do our best living now, today, in the present tense. With this thought firmly before us, we are further challenged to…

Taking Charge of Our Own Actions

To do our best living in the present tense is what every thinking, responsible Christ follower desires. In order to do so, we must, under the Father's guidance, take charge of our own actions, as well as our reactions.

I recall when this truth sank into my soul. Some years ago, I was reading my favorite newspaper columnist in our morning newspaper. He described taking a friend with him to his office on a routine morning. They stopped, as was the columnist's custom, to buy a newspaper at the newsstand in the lobby of his office building. The shopkeeper was gruff and irritable.

"Is the shopkeeper always that way?" asked the friend. "Unfortunately, yes," replied the columnist. His friend, somewhat offended by this behavior, persisted, "Then why don't you just tell him off? Or maybe avoid him?" The columnist answered, "Because I am not going to let *him* decide how *I* behave."

Now that was not a prescribed "spiritual" situation. It was everyday life. However, it shows how spiritual principles apply to *all* of life—to every hour of every day.

"So then, each of us will give an account of himself to God."
                                                    —Romans 14:12

Therefore, we must not let others determine how *we* behave! Because we will be giving an accounting to God, we must take charge of our own actions *and* reactions. Those who blame others for their own chosen actions and reactions have shallow, malnourished souls. They are like the little boy who said, "The fight started when he hit me back."

"Not my brother, not my sister, but it's me, O Lord," and it's each of us who is responsible for our own behavior and attitudes, regardless of what the rest of the world is doing. What freedom there is when we take this spiritual dimension into the depth of our beings.

A True Story

There is an old, but true, story told by Alfred Adler about two men who encountered one another years ago in a train station in Austria. One was an alcoholic who approached a well-dressed businessman and asked for enough money to buy a bottle of wine.

Before responding to the request, the businessman asked the beggar with genuine interest how such an intelligent-looking man had come to the place of living from one drink to the next. The beggar answered that he had had a very hard life. Things had gone awry and the cards of life had been stacked against him.

He explained that his mother died when he was very young, and his father was a cruel man who had beaten him and his siblings mercilessly. Then World War I had caused the entire family to be separated from one another, and there was no one who cared about him. Then he said, "I never had a chance. If you'd grown up like I did, you'd be this way, also."

The businessman paused, and then said, "This is amazing, for the very same events happened to me. But as I thought about it, and reflected on my alternatives, I decided to try to overcome those negative circumstances and bad breaks."

The two men continued to talk and finally made a startling discovery. They were brothers, long separated by the War. They had identical circumstances in their backgrounds, but they responded very differently.

Dr. George Buttrick observed this truth: "The same sun that hardens clay melts wax." His statement is another acknowledgement of the importance of reaction in the unfolding of events and life experiences. There is indeed action, but there is also *reaction*, or response. Clay and wax have no choice in the way they react to the sun, but we human beings can choose our reactions to the heat of life.

The question arises surprisingly often: Will we be wax, and respond to what happens by inviting God, in all His creativity, to soften us and reshape us into Christlikeness? Or will we be clay, and allow the circumstances to harden our souls and make us brittle, turning our backs on the Father's loving desire to redeem us and provide us His close guidance? Every one of us has this same choice to make, in small ways and large ways, throughout our lives.

Be Equally at Ease with Life and Death

God is pleased when we choose to do our best living in the present tense, taking charge of our own reactions, for this prepares us to be at ease with life or death. We need that ease. Ease with death? Really? Yes! Paul wrote to the Philippians:

"For to me, living means opportunities for Christ, and dying—well that's better yet!"
—Philippians 1:21 TLB

Paul was in prison awaiting trial as he wrote this well-known letter to his friends in Philippi. He did not know whether he would live or be condemned to die. Actually, to him, it made no difference. How amazing!

His remarkable message was that there is one thing even better than living as a Christ follower on planet earth. That is to die and spend forever with the living, reigning Christ in person! In other words, to *live* is Christ, and to *die* is even better! Eugene Peterson's paraphrase of this verse makes it resound even more beautifully in our hearts:

"Alive, I'm Christ's messenger; dead, I'm his bounty. Life versus even more life! I can't lose."
—Philippians 1:21 *The Message*

I love this quotation from Dr. Carl Henry: "Death is transition from life to life."

This means that the end of life is *not* the end of life!

I want to live and die with these convictions. Doing our best living in the present tense is a spiritual dimension that stabilizes our souls as it transforms our days. Transformed days add up to *quality* life with God and others. A quality life in the present tense allows us to go to bed at night feeling good about the day, keeping the lines clear and wide open to hearing His voice, His call, His guidance. Priceless!

A Sure Thing: Death

Perhaps I should be more subtle, but a sure thing in this world is—except for those who are living when Christ returns—100 percent of us will die. Therefore, it makes sense to give attention, not only to how to live well, but also to how to die well.

We often hear references to "the art of living." Leonard Sweet challenges his readers in his book *Soul Salsa* to plan to go out in a blaze of glory by mastering what the ancients called the art of dying. Dying!? Sweet calls it "the art of happy endings." I like that phrase.

Sweet makes a number of suggestions designed to help master "the art of happy endings." I am fascinated by his musings. To me, his thoughts seem to be applicable to our lives long *before* the "endings" of life. In other words, let's not wait until we are old and gray and/or on our deathbeds to seriously consider his suggestions! In fact, my personal desire is to do these very things *now*, in the present tense, whenever and wherever appropriate, regardless of my age.

~ Tell stories to nearby loved ones and visitors about the divine coherences in your life. You won't understand all of what God intended for your life until you've gained the perspective of Abraham's bosom. However, the deathbed isn't a bad place either to trace the working of God in your life—and to testify about it to those around you.

~ Commission heirs, bless the succeeding generations, bestow your mantle, bequeath your treasures. When the patriarchs were dying, they established both the birthright and the blessings—material and spiritual legacies that would outlast them.

~ Set the past straight. What threads are dangling that you need to tie up? Do so. Now.

~ Make peace with God and with others around you. Do so. Now. Whatever your age and stage.

See what I mean? These have to do not only with the ending of life on earth, but with the way we live in the present tense.

Sweet concludes, "How long our genetic whirlpool will allow all our cells to talk to each other and work together is anyone's guess and God's surprise. But one day an organism will lose the struggle against a competing organism. Disease has functions as well as causes—the germ wins, the body dies."

O Death, Where Is Your Sting?

Of course, the Christ follower does not really die. The germ does not really win. Yes, death has meaning for the body, but the life of the soul is everlasting. Our souls will never "know" death. Therefore, death, where is your sting?

If we have sought to live our lives, day by day, in a way that brings glory to God and service to others, then we can exclaim with Paul:

"Death swallowed by triumphant Life! Who got the last word, oh, Death? Oh, Death, who's afraid of you now?"

—1 Corinthians 15:54–55 *The Message*

Although I am convinced that death needs an appropriate amount of our attention, this discussion has more to do with life than with death. We must acknowledge again and again the absolute importance of every day of our lives *on earth.* Each day is so essential because God calls every one of His people to do certain specific things that make a difference in this life and in this world—today!

"We make a living by what we get, but we make a life by what we give."

—Winston Churchill

"A disciplined follower of Jesus is someone who discerns when laughter, gentleness, silence, healing words, or prophetic indignation is called for, and offers it promptly, effectively, and lovingly."

—John Ortberg

pathway
eleven

LIVE A LIFE
OF
GRATITUDE

"Give thanks in all circumstances, for this is God's will for you in Christ Jesus."

—1 Thessalonians 5:18

"Trust the Lord and sincerely worship him; think of all the tremendous things he has done for you."

—1 Samuel 12:24 TLB

We have acknowledged the power to choose our own reactions as a tremendous privilege God has given to us. Our choices make a difference in the content of our days. Simply and clearly stated, the Bible insists that choosing a lifestyle of thanksgiving is a must. Paul declares that we are to "give thanks in all circumstances." This is indeed God's will for every Christ follower—a necessary pathway to follow in the journey toward Christlikeness. We do not have the liberty of being ungrateful.

⊿s it possible for us—or anyone—to always give thanks in all circumstances? Is this admonition realistic?

Thankful Even in a Time of Trouble

In reflecting on Paul's insistence that we be thankful in *all* circumstances, think back to his own experiences. He was in at least three shipwrecks. We know of multiple times when he was beaten with a rod. Five times, he received 39 lashes. Also, Paul was bitten by a snake, stoned, and often imprisoned. Indeed, Paul had his share of grief. Yet he wrote so clearly and emphatically about being thankful.

We are quick to acknowledge that "a life of gratitude" is not an easy pathway to take. As we find ourselves confronted with pain, grief, and distress, the questions slip into our consciousness, "Why did this happen to me? How can I possibly be thankful here and now?"

Many say in such moments, "Life is not fair. Why me?" Others say, "Life is totally fair, for life breaks everyone's heart."

Both statements contain elements of truth. Indeed, no one in this world is immune to burdens and heartbreaks. We are all "acquainted with grief." However, the power God gives us to choose our own reactions (we are back to that again!) *does* make it possible to live a life of gratitude. Actually, it is His power within us that frees us from a festering focus on those circumstances that go awry and break our hearts.

Give Thanks in the Midst of All Circumstances

The Father's straightforward intention is for us to give thanks *in* all circumstances. Notice Paul did not say we are to give thanks *for* all circumstances. He counseled the Thessalonian Christ followers to have a grateful attitude in the *midst* of all circumstances. There is a difference between *in* and *for* all circumstances.

Certainly there are situations for which we are not asked to be thankful—those involving sin and evil, for example. Yet even in the unfolding of negative circumstances for which we cannot be honestly grateful, we can be quietly and legitimately thankful for our Lord's utter dependability in using even our pain and disappointments to grow us to be more like Jesus— the highest goal of the Christ-following life, the essence of spirituality. This is God's will for us: to focus on the positive good He does within us, even in the midst of, and as the result of, our heartbreak. To whatever degree we allow Him to be at work within us and within our circumstances, He is amazingly redemptive. We can trust Him. He will not let us down.

Indeed, God's will for us is to be authentically grateful *in the midst of everything*—whatever the circumstances. Granted, I know for certain this is not easy. I have struggled with this principle myself. But I take my stand that, with God's help, it can be done. God calls us to be grateful.

Name Our Blessings One by One

I find additional understanding in bringing to my mind again and again an Old Testament verse:

"Trust the Lord and sincerely worship him; think of all the tremendous things he has done for you."

—1 Samuel 12:24 TLB

When I pause and meditate on the tremendous things our Lord *already* has done for me, and observe His creative power at work in the lives of those I know and care about close at hand and around the world, I find my heart filled to over-flowing with genuine worship and thanksgiving. At some point in this process, gratitude overflows my soul.

To live true to the biblical principle from 1 Samuel mentioned above, we are to keep our hearts set continually on those "tremendous things" God has done for us. Naming our specific blessings impresses upon us His goodness, love, grace, mercy, and generosity. We keep in mind that every-thing, even our heartbreak—*especially* our heartbreak—goes through His hands. Because of His power and creativity, He can redeem *every* circumstance, tragedies included, and even bring "little Easters" out of them for us.

Being thankful contributes to contentment in any and every state. Paul wrote to the Philippians,

"I have learned how to be content...in whatever state I am."
—Philippians 4:11 AMP

On a lighter note, some Texans I know are quick to comment that this verse proves Paul was *not* a Texan! If he had been, some Texans say, Paul would not have been able to make this statement. Seriously, what a wonderful discovery to learn that we can choose our "state." Therefore, choose to live in the state of contentment and gratitude. It is a blessed state.

We Choose Our Own Perspective

A related matter that builds a foundation of joyful gratitude is the choice of a positive perspective. This calls for us to choose to place the best possible *realistic* construction on situations and people.

"Summing it all up, friends, I'd say you'll do best by filling your minds and meditating on things true, noble, reputable, authentic, compelling, gracious—the best, not the worst; the beautiful, not the ugly; things to praise, not things to curse."

—Philippians 4:8 *The Message*

To apply this biblical instruction to our everyday situations and relationships can be revolutionary. This is a generalization, but generally speaking, everyone reading these words is predominately positive or predominately negative. We tend either to focus downward on the mud, or look up at the stars. My mother used to quote the following lines:

"Two men looked out from prison bars;
One saw mud, the other, stars."

My mother's lines do make an important point. Even as one person chooses to look up and the other chooses to look down, this same choice is ours to make many times a day. We can look at the mud, sound a sour note, express a negative feeling. Or we can look up, choose an upbeat note to sound as we take a positive perspective.

Which are you—predominantly positive or predominantly negative?

One who is predominantly negative emits a poison that infects a marriage, a family, a committee, a church, an office, a class. It is a destructive power, defying God's intention for His people. Have you heard it said, "She can light up a room—by leaving it!" On the other hand, one who is realistically positive naturally emits hope, encouragement, affirmation. This person says with the poet Robert Browning,

"The best is yet to be,
The last of life, for which the first was made."

How true. The best of life is yet to be for those who choose to live a life of gratitude and contentment, those who look up with a positive perspective, and say "Thank you, Lord."

Let us be reminded again of the importance of the daily discipline to meditate on all the tremendous things God has done for us. This is the pathway to living a life of gratitude. And living a life of gratitude is a pathway to Christlikeness.

I am always moved by these simple words of Dag Hammarskjöld, which I mentioned earlier. He prayed,

"For all that has been, thanks.
For all that will be, yes!"

**$\mathcal{L}$ord, I want to live with these words daily
in my soul and on my lips. Amen.**

*pathway
twelve*

THINK—REFLECT—
PONDER

*"Don't become so well-adjusted to your culture that you fit into it
without even thinking. Instead, fix your attention on God. You'll be
changed from the inside out."*
—Romans 12:2 *The Message*

*"You were taught, with regard to your former way of life, to put off
your old self…to be made new in the attitude of your minds."*
—Ephesians 4:22–23

*"Summing it all up, friends, I'd say you'll do best by filling your
minds and meditating on things true, noble, reputable, authentic,*

compelling, gracious—the best, not the worst; the beautiful, not the
ugly; things to praise, not things to curse."

—Philippians 4:8 *The Message*

A unique, basic fact of life is that God created human beings with minds, the capacity to think. In fact, the mind has been called the "steering wheel" of the person. Indeed, transformation into the likeness of Christ does not take place without a continuing renewing of our minds. This means that the thoughts we allow to enter our minds are of utmost importance in negotiating the pathway to Christlikeness.

We have heard all our lives, "What we think is who we are." Do we really believe this old maxim? The Scriptures certainly affirm its truth. We must think in ways that will give us insight into the mind of Christ and point us to His way of thinking.

I am convinced that many of us do not give adequate time and thought to our magnificent God-given ability to think and reflect. Too often, we stay on the surface of life, making decisions that come "off the top of our heads" without being thoroughly examined in our minds and hearts. Too often, this leads to decisions and actions that result in much regret. I know I need to slow down and give mental and spiritual effort to focusing my mind on those situations and relationships that are confusing and complex. I need to ask the Father to think His thoughts through me and give me *His* mind, *His* "take" on matters that need my thoughtful, thorough attention.

Paul wrote to the Christ followers living in Colosse: "Set your minds on things above" (Colossians 3:2). Is this not good advice for us as well?

When Our Thinking Is Muddled

We are very aware of "quandary" times—those times when we are muddled about what we think or feel. When the situation before us is gray instead of black or white, there can be confusion about what our actions should be. The primary way for setting our minds on things above, of working through a time of confusion, is in focusing on the presence of our heavenly Father. I know from experience that when I keep my appointment with Him, often there comes to my attention from out of the blue a thought, an insight, an understanding, a solution, or an action that needs to be factored into the mix of the situation. It typically rings the bell of being God's direct answer for me.

My preference for such a time of reflection and pondering alone with the Father is when I am doing my daily exercise, walking over the dale and through the woods. It is then that I intentionally plan to bring a certain confusing subject or situation to my mind and to the Father's full attention. It seems to me that my walking time somehow lends itself to this level of creative thinking with the Lord—seeking to know His mind through my intentional reflecting and pondering. As I breathe deeply the beauty of His creation, freshly aware of His love, provision, power, and sovereignty, my mind seems to clear, and joins my heart in worship of our living, reigning Lord. Many times, I make my way back to my nest with a breakthrough thought or understanding the Father has given me. Almost without exception, my ponderings with Him and worship of Him have brought, in addition to fresh thinking to my mind, a refreshment to my soul.

What Is "Thinking?"

Dallas Willard gives extraordinary guidance on the importance of the mind and its transformation in both *The Divine*

Conspiracy and *The Renovation of the Heart.* In his latest book, *The Renovation of the Heart*, he gives an enlightening description of thinking as well as a statement of its purpose:

> What is thinking? Thinking is the activity of searching out what *must* be true, or *cannot* be true, in the light of given facts or assumptions. It extends the information we have and enables us to see the "larger picture," to see it clearly and to see it wholly. And it undermines false or misleading ideas and images as well. It reveals their falseness to those who wish to know. It is a powerful gift of God to be used in the service of truth....The prospering of God's cause on earth depends upon his people thinking well.

Thinking Well—How Does It Develop?

We should be quick to acknowledge that we get our clearest thinking from the Scriptures.

"The revelation of GOD is whole and pulls our lives together. The signposts of GOD are clear and point out the right road. The life-maps of GOD are right, showing the way to joy. The directions of GOD are plain and easy on the eyes. GOD's reputation is twenty-four-carat gold, with a lifetime guarantee. The decisions of GOD are accurate down to the nth degree."

—Psalm 19:7–9 *The Message*

I need continually to keep myself reminded of God's words, to keep "enlightening my eyes" (see Ephesians 1:18), and thus feeding my mind and heart with the thoughts and precepts of the Master. This is the pathway to thinking well.

Our Thinking Leads to What We *Do*

What we *think,* of course, has a way of determining what we *do.* Generally speaking (although there are exceptions), each of our actions begins with a thought. It may be only the *beginning* of a thought, which abruptly leads to an impulsive action. However, the thought usually takes quick form and shape in our minds a split second (at least) before we act.

The exceptions have to do with those who do not think at all before they act or make decisions. They are victims of their own breakdown in elementary discipline and judgment. When asked, "What were you thinking when you did (or said) that?" they answer, "I was just not thinking at all." How sad. God gave us minds and a marvelous ability to think, reflect, and ponder, but many fail to use their minds as a treasured part of God's guidance.

We must take time to think through what we believe from God's Word and Jesus' teachings. Then, using "consecrated common sense," we base our action (doing) upon the direction our surrendered minds have received from God and His wisdom.

Our Goal: To Think Like Jesus Thinks

Christlikeness calls us to think like Jesus thinks. Thus, basic to the Christ-following life is the continual transformation of our minds to be more like His mind—an awesome thought in itself!

Review again Romans 12:2. We are challenged by Scripture to avoid the temptation to adjust our thinking to the culture that surrounds us. How timely—sounds as though Paul wrote his letter to us today! We are being bombarded with messages to think like the world thinks. Television, movies, and related magazines have tremendous impact on the thinking of a large percentage of Americans. Generally, our culture promotes everyone being "turned loose" to pick and choose (and even make up) their *own* truths, and their own pathways.

Every one of us has the power to select what we will allow into our minds. Colossians 3:2 reminds us to set our minds on things above. The "above" matters require thinking, pondering, reflecting on God's Word, and thoughtfully listening to the still, small voice of His Holy Spirit. It means to think realistically and positively, to think thankfully, to do our best thinking and living today, in the present tense. It means to move down all the pathways we are discussing in these pages.

In *The Renovation of the Heart,* Dallas Willard further observes, "As our senses present a landscape for our body and its actions, so our thoughts present the 'lifescape' for our will and our life as a whole. Within that 'thought lifescape' (including our perceptions) we make the decisions that determine what we will do and who we will become."

A major question confronting us is: "Will we choose to have God as a constant presence in our minds?" We must decide whether or not we will allow Him to determine the subject matter of our thoughts or else give that power to the world and its influences.

The Ultimate Freedom

Perhaps the ultimate freedom we have in this world is to choose what we will allow and/or require our minds to dwell upon. In the light of this truth, the ultimate goal of the Christ follower is to dwell upon those matters that lead to knowing Him intimately, to understanding His teachings, His thinking, His heart. In the midst of life's dilemmas, confusions, and ultimate questions, let us thank God for the marvelous gift of our minds. Let us ask Him to fill them with His thoughts as we think—reflect—ponder.

*pathway
thirteen*

BLESS EVERYONE
YOU ENCOUNTER

"Be kind and compassionate to one another."

"Be gentle with one another, sensitive."
—Ephesians 4:32 NIV and *The Message*

The first Bible verse many of us learned was, "Be ye kind" (Ephesians 4:32 KJV). It may be that if Paul were writing to us today, he would say "Bless everyone you encounter."

A blessing can be as simple as just plain caring, giving respect, being patient, expressing gentle, affirming words and actions. Blessing someone is being sensitive to the current situation in which we as Christ followers find ourselves. A blessing "happens" when the fruit of the Spirit is exhibited in one's actions.

I am sad to admit this, but I have seen many Christians act in unkind ways. Are they *faking* their spirituality? Of course, this is not for you or me to even take a guess, but we cannot help but notice their "fruit." Actually, when I observe an unkindness, my commitment is to let the observation be a reminder for me to do a reality check on myself!

We should all practice giving a blessing everywhere we go. I had a test of this the other day. I almost flunked. I am going to tell you about it anyway.

My Corner Supermarket

I had dashed into the grocery store to get a few items—quickly. I did not even get a basket for my short list. You know, you have been there. I hurriedly collected my half-dozen purchases and juggled them in my arms as I headed for the "10 items and under" checkout line. There were only two people there, and one was in the midst of being checked out. That was good to see. "This won't take long," I assured myself.

I joined the little scene, and then I realized the young checker was having a problem with the cash register in the middle of his current transaction. He was obviously hassled, and I noticed that his brow was covered with perspiration. I said to myself "He's new...and he's learning...and he's botched up the register...and I need to get into another line and get out of here ASAP."

The lady whose groceries the young man was in the middle of checking was noticeably impatient. The checker was calling customer service for help. The man in front of me took a deep and obvious breath and went to another line.

I started to follow him, but then I stopped. I do believe it was a nudge from the Lord, for the thought came to me that what mattered most in these next few moments was for me to cool my heels and give this young man a blessing. He needed encouragement and a kind word in the midst of his frustration and embarrassment. I took a deep and obvious breath myself and decided to stay with the hung-up checker. In a moment, customer service had the cash register up and working.

The checker began again. He was nervously slow in punching the keys, and by then the perspiration was dripping off his face. I was next. I handed him a Kleenex. I told him to take his time, that he was more important than my groceries or my time. His eyes met mine for the first time, and he visibly relaxed. To tell you the whole truth, he kind of melted.

He said, "I am sorry you had to wait." I assured him it was okay, and told him I had stayed in his line on purpose, just to remind him that there are times when things go awry for all of us, every one of us. He thanked me for understanding and reached out both his hands and took one of mine. He smiled and squeezed my hand with firmness. What a blessing I felt *from him*! I squeezed back.

Who Gets the Bigger Blessing?

I thanked the Lord for His divine nudge. Of course, there is no guarantee a blessing will "connect" with the one for whom it is intended, nor is there a guarantee that it will boomerang back to us. However, I have noticed that usually I wind up getting more of a blessing than the very small one I have given.

Have you heard about the little boy who prayed, "Lord, make all the bad people good, and all the good people, kind"? We don't identify with being "bad" people. But are we consistently, overtly, sensitively kind to everyone we meet?

"Be gentle with one another, sensitive."
—Ephesians 4:32 *The Message*

So just be kind everywhere you turn. Nearly always, the simplest kindness blesses the other person. Most of the time, *you* will receive the larger blessing. Although our motive for blessing others should never be to get blessed in return, it just happens. You have experienced this, and felt the blush of quiet, deep satisfaction while doing the kind thing at the needed time.

Of course, not everyone receives our blessing as a blessing. We still need to give it, to be kind, to bless everyone we encounter, regardless.

~ We especially need to give overt blessings to those closest to us. There are those of us who *appear* to be spiritual but who are least kind and gentle and sensitive to those with whom we have the most contact—our families. It is so easy to take the familiar for granted. Be especially careful to give a daily special blessing (and many more than one) to those with whom you live.

~ Give generous blessings to your fellow church members, also. Your spiritual family is just as needful of your blessing as anyone else. Go out of your way to do so.

~ Add your neighbors to this list. Have you found ways to bless your neighbors? What a testimony this can be. Our neighbor blesses us by putting our morning paper at our front door every morning (except Sundays, when we get up earlier than he does, and Bill places their paper at their front door.)

~ Remember your workplace. Many times a day there are opportunities to do the kind thing, to bless those around you in a wide variety of creative ways.

Mother Teresa is often quoted as having said, "We cannot do great things on this earth. We can only do little things with great love."

One of my favorite stories has to do with the small boy who was awakened in the middle of the night by a thunderstorm. Frightened, he called out for his parents, at the same time making his way to their bedroom for comforting. His father responded with soothing words, "Son, don't be afraid. You know God will take care of you."

"I know God will take care of me," the boy replied, "but I need someone to take care of me who has skin on!"

All of us have that same need. We all—there are no exceptions—need someone (make that plural) to bless us who has skin on. Plus, we need to *be* that someone who has skin on, blessing those we encounter.

$\mathcal{D}$on't forget to just "Be ye kind."

"The person God blesses automatically affects those around him and those who are associated with him."

—Henry Blackaby

"You cannot do a kindness too soon, for you never know how soon it will be too late."

—Ralph Waldo Emerson

REFUSE TO CAMP
IN YOUR WILDERNESS

*T*his chapter doesn't begin with a Scripture quote because I'm using the entire book of Exodus as the basis for this pathway. I am going to change the analogy of our earlier thinking from the sea to the wilderness.

The children of Israel were in the wilderness. God was leading them to make the extraordinary move from years of slavery in Egypt to the Promised Land. Along the way, covering many long years, they met obstacles, hardships, and challenges, one after another, as they "toured" the wilderness.

*C*an you imagine how difficult
it was for them to keep on going?
*C*an you imagine how complex
and trying the logistics were?

*T*he children of Israel were on their way home.
Do you think they were tempted to give up the journey?
Do you think it occurred to them somewhere along the
way, in the midst of those many years, to establish
a new territory and get on with their lives?

Yet God was leading them onward, guiding them with a pillar
of cloud by day and a pillar of fire by night. He provided the
strength they needed day by day in the form of manna. Eventually, after many years and many trying experiences in the
wilderness, they made it to the Promised Land.

A Wilderness at Every Corner

We, too, have wilderness times. We have acknowledged our
wilderness times in various ways as we have referred to our
disappointments, sorrows, hurts, angers, and regrets. We, too,
have a choice, even as the children of Israel did, as to how we
will relate to our times in a wilderness.

We can set up camp and stay right there with those difficult experiences, camping in our own little wildernesses—or
we can move on, following God's guidance, and His day-by-day
provision of nurture for our journey.

I identify strongly with this point. When my late husband died in the prime of his life, our many dreams and plans
were suddenly, traumatically gone. I was devastated. Living
without him felt, in a sense, like wandering in a wilderness,

and this wandering was not for 40 years, but it was for 22 years!

Frankly, it was tempting to set up camp, to gather my dashed dreams around me, and settle down into self-pity. Yet even as I grieved, God was calling me to follow His pillar of cloud by day and His pillar of fire by night. He faithfully gave me enough manna to get through the day and the night—and I am headed for the Promised Land. And He has given me, all through my journey, many "little Easters."

God Leads Us to the Promised Land

Are you camping in a wilderness of an old hurt or loss or self-pity or hostility or unfulfilled expectation or disappointment? Have you refused to budge from a point of resentment and anger in your past? If so, you are camping in your own private wilderness, far from home, from the Promised Land. Yet God is there with you, wanting to lead you to move on and out, following Him and His leadership. As one who has been in the wilderness—as I am sure you have, also—I encourage you to refuse to camp there. Follow His pathways, and He will lead you to the Promised Land.

Are you willing to follow Him "home?"
"I am bound for the Promised Land.
O, who will come and go with me?"

"Relying on God has to begin all over again every day as if nothing had yet been done."
—C. S. Lewis

*pathway
fifteen*

KEEP YOUR
BALANCE

"Watch your step, and the road will stretch out smooth before you."
—Proverbs 4:26 *The Message*

"If he stumbles, he's not down for long; GOD has a grip on his hand."
—Psalm 37:24 *The Message*

can testify to the importance of balance. Several years ago, I lost mine. I mean, I *really* lost it. I tripped and made a major effort to "catch myself" in the midst of my stumbling. However, after staggering a half dozen or so awkward steps, I lost the rest of my remaining balance, and went down. Hard. Real hard. I don't recommend it.

After about half an hour, I admitted to myself that something was wrong with my left arm. I drove myself to the emergency room and went through their rigmarole. Eventually, the emergency room doctor reported to me that the X-rays revealed my fall had created a hairline fracture in my humeral head. I did not even know I had one—and actually, I have two!

My Humeral Head in a Sling

The doctor put my arm in a comfortable sling and told me to go to an orthopedic doctor to have follow-up X-rays in four weeks. My children already had planned a long weekend celebration of my 70th birthday in New York City. We diagnosed that my slightly messed up humeral head would not need to affect our trip, since my arm did not bother me at all. We forged ahead with our plans, and had a super good time on our celebrative outing. I even enjoyed the occasional pampering the sling brought me. We did everything we were scheduled to do. This humeral head thing had turned out to be a breeze.

Shortly after we returned, it was time to see the orthopedist. His x-rays revealed that my humeral head had healed nicely. Then the doctor prescribed 10 weeks of physical therapy, to begin immediately. The purpose was to regain full use of my left arm, which had been comfortably immobile, of course, for a month. I did not have time to add those lengthy twice-a-week therapy sessions to my schedule. However, I soon learned that the time involved was not my biggest problem.

My biggest problem was the physical therapy clinic— which turned out to be a torture chamber. Those therapists were super nice guys, but they hurt me big time. I tried to make all kinds of deals with them. I even offered to bring them a homemade cake—if they would give me a break from their painful routines. Well, they did ease up a little on the day I brought the cake, but by and large, they had no mercy. Belatedly, I keenly suffered the consequences of having lost my balance.

On Losing One's Spiritual Balance

Of ultimately more importance than the physical balance of the Christ follower is the matter of spiritual balance. When we lose our balance spiritually, there are even more serious consequences, although at first it may appear that we have been able to skip the negative outcomes. Like my arm and its humeral head, the long-term consequences can be dramatically more painful than the immediate ones. My arm demonstrated that this truth was holding firm. There seems to be an unseen but permeating law: there *is* a payday, someday. I intend *not* to forget this recent lesson.

My experience caused me to think and reflect at length. Actually, my thoughts had nothing to do with my humeral head. I discovered I had some balancing to do in my *life*. I have difficulty keeping my balance when it comes to the use of my time, for example. I have already shared my commitment to give an appropriate portion of my day (or late evening) to solitary time with God. Also, I give a certain amount of time to the people and responsibilities included in my commitments. When this gets out-of-kilter, the problem may not be obvious to the casual bystander, but like my humeral head, it takes its toll in unseen (and sometimes seen) ways. Again, there is a payday, someday. I prefer to avoid those days.

Another of the rhythms of life that needs to be in balance is the combination of work and recreation. Balance is never simple to achieve. Most of us lean more toward one extreme or the other. Without a doubt, we need to be reliable and productive, but we also need to respect the place of rest and recreation.

There is a tendency to be impressed with the "dedication" of those who work an inordinate amount of time. However, if one is truly out of balance, sooner or later, consequences will catch up. Tripping and landing on one's humeral head could possibly be the result! We all need to withdraw regularly, and be quiet and still or do whatever will recreate us and restore balance to our lives. Let this be a slight, familiar reminder that we must balance work and recreation appropriately.

Respecting the Rhythms of Life

Specifically, as a Christ follower, I need to invest appropriate amounts of my energy in and with my family. Their needs and preferences must be respected, treasured, and enjoyed. This means also that I must have alone times as well. Too much of either togetherness or aloneness is ill advised.

We need to work toward balance with those with whom we have commitments for closeness. These commitments are a supremely important part of the appropriate rhythms of life.

Do you feel unbalanced? Take stock, and determine
what aspect of your life is in need of rebalancing.
Jesus is our model. We are to be like Him.
This is an important pathway to Christlikeness.

pathway
sixteen

BECOME AND
STAY PHYSICALLY FIT

*"Didn't you realize that your body is a sacred place, the place of
the Holy Spirit? Don't you see that you can't live however you
please, squandering what God paid such a high price for? The
physical part of you is not some piece of property belonging to the
spiritual part of you. God owns the whole works. So let people see
God in and through your body."*

—1 Corinthians 6:19–20 *The Message*

The apostle Paul clearly explained to "the church of
God in Corinth, to those sanctified in Christ Jesus
and called to be holy, together with all those everywhere who

call on the name of our Lord Jesus Christ" (1 Corinthians 1:2) that our physical bodies are sacred. I would like to emphasize again the scriptural base of this pathway as Paul expressed so eloquently in our opening Scripture.

I am aware there are some spiritually-minded folks who believe the physical part of our beings barely registers, if at all, as a spiritual matter. My spiritually-minded parents, in fact, felt decidedly different. They agreed with Paul that this matter of the physical is, indeed, a situation with clear spiritual ramifications.

The Spirituality of the Physical

My folks were religious about the food we ate and the exercise we took. *Religious* was the appropriate word then, whereas today *spiritual* would be, no doubt, the more current term to use. My earliest memories relate to my dad's exercising— meaning plain ol' calisthenics—and then doing daily, vigorous walking as well. The importance of fitness of the body was instilled in me in ways I cannot exactly describe—maybe osmosis. In retrospect, my parents were decades ahead of their time in their attention to being physically fit. Daddy claimed to have ordered the first electric juicer (to extract fresh orange and grapefruit juices from the fruit, and also to make delicious carrot and celery juices!) to find its way to San Antonio.

Growing up in a neighborhood of all boys and no girls, back in the days when our playmates were our neighborhood kids, I had to join the boys in their activities, or else I did not have playmates. There was no way they would join me in my game of croquet! Thus, I played their very active sports with them. I must admit I did not mind. I enjoyed all the stuff they played—even football and pole vaulting! As a teenager, my interests changed dramatically, and I swore off those guy-type activities. As a young adult, I took up tennis and that became my exercise of choice for close to half a century.

My point is that my parents instilled in me the importance of exercise decades before the current era of strong emphasis on physical fitness. Even now, I walk three miles every day I possibly can, weather-wise and schedule-wise. I cherish the time, and try to arrange it to coincide with the setting of the sun. When the weather prevents my walking, I "do" my Nordic Track. I am not crazy about the contraption, but I try to do one form of exercise or the other.

Is Food Really a Spiritual Matter?

Food was also a spiritual matter at my house. Frankly, I did not like my mother's cooking. She never fried *anything*. I mean, nothing. She did not believe in eating fried foods of any kind. Neither did my dad. Except for ice cream and fruit, they did not allow desserts. I thought it was like heaven-is-bound-to-be when we were invited "out to eat" by our church members. This always meant a cobbler or something sweet and sugary and almost as wonderful as cobblers.

I had to grow up to appreciate the wisdom of my parents. Although I have not risen to their level of dedication to the principles of exercise and eating right (in fact, I'm a slouch compared to them!), I did turn into an adult who was greatly impacted by their staunch insistence on the benefits of health-wise beliefs and practices.

In retrospect, somehow I knew (even then) they were right. Although I make cracks about my upbringing, I feel very indebted to my parents and to the Lord for my current energy level at this advanced age and stage in my life. My mother lived to the age of 83, and my dad was two months short of 102 at the time of his death. He, especially, did *something* right!

Another emphasis in my growing up years was the proper amount of sleep. This I did fairly well as a teenager. In fact, I was called a sleepyhead, for I loved to sleep 'till noon on Saturdays. I would have liked to have slept in on other days also, but I was not allowed to discover how good that could be!

It seemed only a few months between the time my parents taught me and my attempt to teach my own children the very same healthy habits of eating, exercise, and rest. Of course, it's been decades, and now my children are teaching their children. It all happened so quickly! I certainly have lived a sufficient number of years to see the importance of leaving a legacy of being physically fit. I have benefited from the legacy left to me.

Like other truths, it is possible to understand this life principle and yet fail to practice it in life. This is the challenge of taking this pathway, to apply God-honoring habits as a part of the wholeness of life in Christ, and thus, reap the benefits.

The bottom line of this is that our physical beings are a gift from God to be cared for and valued. Indeed, keeping our bodies fit is a biblical principle. The spiritual challenge is to care for them in a way that is pleasing to the Father, for our bodies are the temples of His Holy Spirit, and we are to honor and serve God with them. At whatever age we are, regardless of our health history, *now* is the time to be faithful to this pathway to Christlikeness.

Physical Well-Being and Spiritual Vitality

The relationship between our physical beings and our spiritual nature is closely interconnected, and even intermingled. Problems related to our physical health, like problems in our spiritual health, are so much easier to prevent than they are to fix. This fact leads the Christ follower to be sensitively concerned about the wellness of one's total being. Neither aspect is to be neglected. Each is influential over the other. God's ideal is health, period. Both spiritual and physical health are pathways to authentic spirituality.

"Therefore, I urge you, brothers, in view of God's mercy, to offer your bodies as living sacrifices, holy and pleasing to God—this is you spiritual act of worship."
—Romans 12:1

Paul's words re-emphasize God's view that our bodies are not only a physical matter, but of spiritual consequence as well. The apostle John also makes a connection between our physical well-being and our spiritual vitality:

"Dear friend, I pray that you may enjoy good health and that all may go well with you, even as your soul is getting along well."
—3 John 1:2

We find various messages in the Bible related to health. The book of Proverbs links emotions to physical health: *"A cheerful heart is good medicine, but a crushed spirit dries up the bones"* (Proverbs 17:22). The Psalms also bear testimony of how guilt over wrongdoing takes its toll on physical, spiritual, and emotional health. Admitting his serious sins, the psalmist wrote, *"When I kept silent, my bones wasted away through my groaning all day long. For day and night your hand was heavy upon me; my strength was sapped as in the heat of summer"* (Psalm 32:3–4).

Decisions and Consequences

Indeed, life is a massive collection of decisions, choices, and the consequences that follow. There is always the temptation to make our decisions without weighing in the relentless impact set in motion by our seemingly inconsequential, everyday choices.

Our bodies become another high-profile illustration of the importance of deciding in advance what we want to achieve, and then setting in motion the actions that move us toward that goal. Often we have to make a choice, knowing we will not reap *now* the results we want. The choice is made in the present, but as in all areas, the desired goal is not achieved until later. In the meantime, hard work is required, and sometimes even discomfort and the pain of discipline are necessary in order to enjoy the gain. Consistent discipline is required as we apply this principle, not only to our physical fitness, but also to every area of our lives and relationships— physical, mental, social, and spiritual.

A Non-Negotiable Life Principle

This is another spiritual life principle to teach our children and youth—whomever God gives us opportunity to influence. Like other truths, it is possible to understand this life principle and yet fail to practice it in the details of our days. This is our challenge: to apply this truth to our lives as a part of the wholeness of life in Christ.

In his book *Ten Essentials of Highly Healthy People*, Dr. Walt Larimore states:

> The biblical view on health can be summed up with the word *blessed*. Blessedness is a theme in the Old Testament and is most clearly described in the New Testament in Jesus' Sermon on the Mount. The Bible makes

the bold assertion that people who aren't socially, financially, physically or mentally gifted can be blessed by God, not rejected by him, and as a result their overall health is enhanced.

Our overall health depends not just on our physical health, important as that is, but also on our inner life. It is this inner emotional and spiritual life that God most wants to nourish and promote, for he knows that without spiritual and emotional well-being, we are less healthy than we were designed to be.

Dr. Larimore makes it clear that being truly healthy is not dependent on physical well-being alone. It includes every area of our being during every stage of our lives. It means being balanced in multiple areas: (1) body, (2) mind, (3) spirit, and (4) community—what Dr. Larimore calls the four "wheels" of health. In balancing these four aspects of health, we become "blessed" and thus, highly healthy.

A major point of blessedness comes into play and extends to others, when out of the bounty of our wellness and fitness, we have the energy and stamina to actively and joyfully move forward on our pathways to Christlikeness. What greater privilege is there?

"Human wholeness or health is a main topic of the Bible. It is only when human beings are whole and their relationships right that they can be described as truly healthy."

—Medical missionary John Wilkinson

pathway
seventeen

TAKE CHRIST SERIOUSLY AND HAVE FUN DOING IT

"A cheerful heart does good like medicine."

—Proverbs 17:22 TLB

"Our mouths were filled with laughter, our tongues with songs of joy."

—Psalm 126:2

can almost hear some readers saying, "Wait a minute! How does *fun* sneak into a book about pursuing the depths of God? Isn't this concept somewhat out of place here?" Well, the word does not just *sneak* in. I believe that fun is a significant aspect of the life committed to following Christ.

In fact, we have been considering many ways of taking Christ seriously. What a privilege and a challenge to be a committed follower of His and have His remarkable resources available for the living of every day. As we have been emphasizing many pathways for the Christ follower to take, some might be thinking, "Hey, that's a long list of heavy stuff! If I take on all of those pathways, and take them seriously, I will be worn out!"

Serious Discipleship and Delightful Fun

This pathway represents one more significant concept in the Christ-following life—having fun as we are taking Christ seriously in our quest for Christlikeness. Fun, playfulness, and rest are indeed elements of well-rounded spirituality. In other words, we constantly *need* these elements in the midst of our daily lives. We are called to take Christ seriously and have a wonderful time doing it!

Fun, playfulness, and rest are necessary antidotes to tiredness and burnout. The folks I know who are serious about following Christ give themselves generously in service to others. Some even overdo their serving. Remember that none of us are superhuman. This may go without saying, but some of us live as though it needs to be said! Also, unfortunately, there are Christians who have never learned *how* to relax and play. Their consciences are overactive and can make them feel like play and fun are not "spiritual," but shallow. They live in the midst of a typical workaholic syndrome—with flashes of guilt and inhibitions in regard to activities that draw them into "just plain fun."

We must carefully respect the way
God made us, for work *and* play.

It is a great challenge in today's hectic, hurried, frantic world to take Christ seriously, and at the same time, to experience an extraordinary measure of joy in doing so.

Having Fun in the Prayer Office

When I was serving as director of the Office of International Prayer Strategy at the (then) Foreign Mission Board of the Southern Baptist Convention, I would jokingly say to my little staff, "We are having entirely too much fun for this to be the Prayer Office!" Let me hasten to add that my coworkers were efficient, effective, and productive. They did their work superbly for the Lord. Our goal was to take Christ seriously, and at the same time, we had a lot of hilarity doing it!

Are you fun to live with? Work with?
Do you hear God calling you to take
Christ seriously and enjoy it?

Rest as a Form of "Play"

I don't know about you, but I consider rest as a form of play. I have not always thought so. Let me explain.

I have told you about my parents' strictness at various points. Another area of their insistence was that I take a nap every Sunday afternoon. In my childhood home, Sunday afternoon naptime seemed to be inherent in one of the Ten Commandments. A part of keeping the sabbath "holy," my mother and father seemed to believe, involved taking a nap.

Even so, I was suspicious that my parents simply wanted a Sunday afternoon nap themselves, and this was their way to put a "holy" sack over our heads—especially mine! As I think about it, naptime really was a part of their religion. Along with *no movies, no shopping,* etc., there was no *fun* on Sunday afternoons—only naps. To me as a child, naps meant torture.

Once I grew up (somewhat), I discovered I *loved* Sunday afternoon naps after all. When I *really* got grown up, I even confessed this to my surprised mom and dad. Excuse me, please, for a little while. This is Sunday, and I need to go take my nap.

Sunday afternoon naps. They are wonderful fun to me now!

Rest Is God's Idea, Not Only My Mom's

Seriously, I am convinced that in our over-extended, frazzled way of life, proper rest is a necessity as well as play. From the Scriptures, we know this is God's thinking. He is the author of the principle of sabbath rest. He set the pattern. He created the earth in six days, and then rested on the seventh. Rest means a time of refreshment, a certain form of renewal, "fun."

Even more importantly, the sabbath (now the Lord's Day) is a day of gathering with God's people for worship and ministry, the day's most significant purpose. The sabbath is a time of renewal and re-creation of the soul and body. Every week, the sabbath calls to our attention the fact that there is more to life than the work we do. Much more.

Christ followers give time and thought to redeeming the Lord's Day. In the last several decades, Sunday has been more and more violated by the secular world. The traditional observance has all but disappeared. Just take a look at the shopping malls' parking lots! Yet Christ followers "Remember the sabbath day, to keep it holy" (Exodus 20:8 KJV). Christ followers give special care and attention to observing the Lord's Day as a special day of bringing honor to Him.

What Is Play by Spiritual Standards?

Let's move from the role of rest to the place of fun in seeking Christlikeness. There are a variety of ways these two aspects can become a natural, normative, joyful, refreshing part of our lives.

There is play we do alone, such as reading, exercise, or our own favorite hobbies. There is play we do with others, in terms of enjoyable conversations, sports, movies, concerts, dining, and any number of delightful activities. In fact, it may be that the most meaningful form of play and fun involves simple, transparent relationships with one or more family members and/or warm friends. This truth certainly rings a bell with me! Indeed, just *being* with special people with whom we can relax is re-creational to our total beings. An invaluable element of warmth and comfort is added to our lives when we spend time with those who have an extra measure of meaning to us.

Taking Christ seriously affirms the giving of one's time and energy to others for helping to meet their needs. Therefore, have fun with those close to you. Especially, have fun with your family. Laughing together is *very* important in the Christ-following home. It echoes in the soul of the family and throughout the home.

Are You Fun to Live With?

How would your family answer this question? Twenty years from now, what will be your children's memories about their childhood? Will they warmly recall fun, laughter, and sweet-ness, or will they remember their early home life as irritable, hectic, conflictive in its atmosphere and relationships, with angry voices prominent in their memories? Stay aware of the necessity to create *today* the memories you want your family and close friends to carry with them the rest of their lives, and the rest of your life as well.

Many of us easily get embroiled and overextended in our constant responsibilities and deadlines. Sometimes we act as though we are indispensable in our roles and work. Some of us can find ourselves working seven days every week. Even as it is spiritual to do our work well and responsibly, we also need periodically to withdraw from work and responsibility. Indeed, withdrawal can also be spiritual, for we are honoring the way God created us and called us to live our everyday lives. Christlikeness leads us to intersperse our work with wholesome play, fun, and also worship.

The Blessing of a Cheerful, Fun Heart

The true Christ follower knows the great blessing of having a cheerful, fun heart—even as we are taking Christ seriously.

In *True Spirituality*, Dr. Francis Schaeffer, noted philosopher, theologian, author, and counselor, wrote,

"A crabbed Christianity is less than orthodox Christianity. …There must be orthodox doctrine, true. But there must also be orthodox *practice* of those doctrines….I hesitate to add, but I will, that this is *fun*. God means Christianity to be fun."

What a delightful statement from this brilliant, distinguished scholar. And what a joyful note for the conclusion of this essential pathway to the depths of God.

176

pathway eighteen

COMMIT YOURSELF TO A LIFESTYLE OF LOVE

(Loving Those Around Us and Throughout the World)

"Regardless of what else you put on, wear love. It's your basic, all-purpose garment. Never be without it."
—Colossians 3:14 *The Message*

"Follow the way of love."
—1 Corinthians 14:1

"Go after a life of love as though your life depended on it—because it does."
—1 Corinthians 14:1 *The Message*

"The entire law is summed up in a simple command: 'Love your neighbor as yourself.'"

—Galatians 5:14

"Love means living the way God commanded us to live. As you have heard from the beginning, his command is this: Live a life of love."

—2 John 1:6 (NCV)

"My command is this: Love each other as I have loved you."

—John 15:12

"Put your life on the line for your friends."

—John 15:13 *The Message*

"For God so loved the world…"

—John 3:16

"Send us around the world with the news of your saving power and your eternal plan for all mankind."

—Psalm 67:2 (TLB)

"Now these three remain: faith, hope and love. But the greatest of these is love."

—1 Corinthians 13:13

*J*esus was, as usual, straightforward and clear. He said the first and greatest commandment is to love God totally and the second one is next in importance: to love others as ourselves. Jesus did not make rash statements. He was saying, "Love is the acid test for the Christ follower."

How easy it is to talk about love! We use the word many times a day. We can go to church every Sunday and do all the spiritual disciplines faithfully. We can obey the Scriptures to the letter of the law. However, if we fail to love and value individuals, not just people in general, then those disciplines are hollow and empty. They become "spiritual cosmetology."

When we fail to love, we fail the Kingdom's most important test and deepest challenge. "Let love be your highest goal" (1 Corinthians 14:1a NLT). Indeed, love is not just *one* of the priorities of the Christian life. Love is the supreme priority.

We have heard this emphasis so much that we can easily be oblivious to its impact and skip to the next thing. Yet it is the "royal law," and we must give our best attention to and perform periodic examination of our current relationship to this priority.

Love's Definition

What, after all, is love? Simply stated, love wants *the best* for the one loved, and is actively involved in bringing that "best" about. Love is an ever-deepening capacity to care for others. Take note that the love Jesus wants us to have for our neighbor is the kind of love alluded to in the "Golden Rule." It is a love that would not wish harm for anyone and that would seek the very best for all mankind.

Jesus taught clearly about this highest priority. Of all His important teachings, His supreme instruction is in the Book of Matthew, where He said in answer to a question about which command in God's laws was most important:

"'Love the Lord your God with all your passion and prayer and intelligence.' This is the most important, the first on any list. But there is a second to set alongside it: 'Love others as well as you love

*yourself.' These two commands are pegs; everything in God's Law
and the Prophets hangs from them."*
—Matthew 22:37–40 The Message

What impressive "pegs." The first and greatest commandment
is to love God with all that we are. Then our love for Him
instills within us a genuine love for others.

Lucy (in the comic strip *Peanuts*) made a famous state-
ment that causes us to smile, even as it has come to be known
as the epitome of non-authenticity. She said, "I love mankind;
It's people I can't stand." I understand, Lucy, for some of us
are not easy to love! Someone has humorously changed the
words to the chorus of the old gospel song "O That Will Be
Glory," to read,

To dwell above, with saints we love,
Oh, that will be glory.
To dwell below with saints we know,
Now, that's another story!

Even as we smile, we know we are dealing with an extremely
serious matter here. We cannot escape this pathway. People
must be loved. Relationships with others are emphasized all
through the Scriptures, and our ability to relate lovingly to
people provides an accurate gauge of our Christlikeness.

Surely we see that God's love is the perfect illustration
of love. Therefore, Kingdom people must make a central com-
mitment to give to others the same compassion, grace, and
mercy—the same love that we have received from Him. We
must pass it on to all mankind. People who love are Kingdom
people.

Love, I learned the hard way, is not only being tender-
hearted (I was okay at that). Real love, Christlike love, is also

tough-minded. Christlike love demands realness and straight-forwardness. Understanding and living out His steady, reliable love in the midst of everyday life is the most important call of the Christ follower's journey. Our greatest challenge is simple, but not easy to fulfill: to live a life of love.

Your Attention, Please

An especially serious test is found in loving and valuing *those closest to us*. Are there people intricately involved in your life who are experiencing your lack of appreciation, your resentment, your withholding of genuine love? If so, there needs to be a serious moment as you consider this failure. Why not take a few minutes just now to reflect on these family relationships?

Our self-examination must begin at home, then encompass our church family, neighbors, coworkers, and reach out to the whole world. God's call to love is clear.

The Pain of Love

We must acknowledge that there is a "backside" of love. No one is immune from this other side, for when we love with Christlike love, we become vulnerable to pain and hurt. Joseph Gallagher writes, "Our human choice is never between pain and no pain, but between the pain of loving and the pain of not loving."

Thus, there is no way to escape pain, whether we love or not. Pain is not an option. Gallagher is right. Again, our choice is never between pain and no pain. It never has been, and never will be.

The questions surface: What kind of pain will we experience? Will it be a form of suffering that goes with loving and making one's self vulnerable to another? Or will it be pain that comes from *not* loving—that agony that accompanies isolation and being cut off?

Suppose we choose the way of love. What happens? Yes, we open ourselves to the possibility (certainty) of hurt and disappointment. At the same time, we open ourselves to relatedness, to being in touch, to having access to life and energy and warmth beyond ourselves.

I can protect myself from pain by not allowing myself to be closely involved with and care deeply about my grandchildren. After all, they have their bumps and hurts and agonies that cause my heart to bleed with and for them. Yet if I should cut myself off from them and their love, I would also cut myself off from a world of joys and all kinds of blessings.

Without exception, we need relatedness and connectedness to others. We could not survive in day-by-day life without the resources that are provided by relationships with others. This is the way God created us from the beginning.

The most acute pain is caused by *not* loving, by attempting to "be myself by myself." Living without loving is a violation of the way God intended us to be—and against all that is taught in His Word.

C. S. Lewis tells of reflecting on what if we get in eternity exactly what we have lived on earth? Lewis is musing on the supposition that if we are loving and giving and caring, we will live eternally in relationships of kind. If we did not give and receive love in our earthly lives, then we would be forever lonely and isolated throughout all eternity. I cannot imagine a greater agony.

In heaven, we will be living with God, Jesus, and others we love and who love us. Hell will be the opposite—void of relationships. Hell is the essence of being cut off, stranded, eternally *lost*.

To Keep on Loving: The Only Choice

As risky as it is, the Christ follower's only choice is to love and keep on loving. That's what Jesus did—and does, and will do throughout all eternity.

I cannot move away from this point without emphasizing again a most positive, even passionate note, about the "rest of the story" concerning love. Even in the midst of the pain of loving, there is joy in love—God's kind of love and His kind of joy. It is a deep, abiding joy that can scarcely be described, but it definitely can be experienced! God pours His love into the heart that is open to following the example of His Son. He gives indescribable joy to those who love Him and day by day, in simple, humble, consistent ways, simply live a life of love.

For God So Loved the World

The Bible's best known, most loved, most memorized verse is John 3:16. God does not only love those who love Him. He loves the whole world, and wants the whole world to come into His arms of love and to the sacrificial love of His "only begotten Son."

"This is how much God loved the world: He gave his Son, his one and only Son. And this is why: so that no one need be destroyed; by believing in him, anyone can have a whole and lasting life. God didn't go to all the trouble of sending his Son merely to point an accusing finger, telling the world how bad it was. He came to help, to put the world right again."

—John 3:16 *The Message*

We have considered the greatest commandment—love. We are to love as God and His Son love—consistently and eternally—everyone. Now let us go where the greatest commandment takes us. It leads us to give our attention to Jesus' Great Commission—and the whole wide world.

The Great Commission and the World

"Jesus came and told his disciples, 'I have been given complete authority in heaven and on earth. Therefore, go and make disciples of all the nations, baptizing them in the name of the Father and the Son and the Holy Spirit. Teach these new disciples to obey all the commands I have given you. And be sure of this: I am with you always, even to the end of the age.'"

—Matthew 28:18–20 (NLT)

"Jesus said to his followers, 'Go everywhere in the world, and tell the Good News to everyone.'"

—Mark 16:15 (NCV)

"You are the light of the world."

—Matthew 5:14

"The field is the world."

—Matthew 13:38

"That God was reconciling the world to himself in Christ, not counting men's sins against them."

—2 Corinthians 5:19

"Send us around the world with the news of your saving power and your eternal plan for all mankind."

—Psalm 67:2 (TLB)

The whole world is very much in the heart of God. Indeed, we are called to "take on" the world and its need for a Savior. The Great Commission is for all of us. God does have a plan in mind for bringing the world to Jesus. His plan includes each of us. He is calling us to think globally.

Our world is shrinking. We are increasingly more connected with the rest of our planet—surrounded with goods that come from many other parts of the globe into our homes. Travel is more common than ever before. More than we ever imagined, we are a mobile people.

Thus, our love *can* reach around the world in multiple ways. Many Kingdom pray-ers are already connected throughout the world through their prayers. Missionaries are constantly enlisting God's people to be a part of their prayer base. Those living and working overseas communicate regularly their specific prayer needs by email—a delightful, meaningful way to be Kingdom pray-ers. Love for God and for lost people has prompted many earnest pray-ers to "put feet to their prayers" by going overseas to bear witness of the wonderful good news of Jesus in person-to-person ways. Many prayerwalking teams go overseas to pray "on site with insight" as they walk and pray with missionaries and/or local Christ followers throughout their areas of ministry and witness. Some prayerwalkers even go to destinations beyond the reach of assigned missionaries to lovingly lift the local people and their need for a Savior heavenward.

Another way to love the people of the world is for volunteers to go overseas for a specific, part-time ministry. In this mobile world, more and more "temporary" ministries can be performed by short-term, Kingdom-loving volunteers. This takes us back to the pathway related to service, and to the matter of discerning our gifts and using them in ministering to and serving others. Isn't it interesting to observe how each pathway has a way of intersecting with other pathways along the way? Hmmmm, if I started connecting all the pathways, I would need to write another book!

Our basic stance as Christ followers must be love. In committing ourselves to a lifestyle of love, we are making ourselves available for God's mission assignment as He "sends us around the world with the news of His saving power and His eternal plan for all mankind" (Psalm 67:2 TLB). God sends us around the world through our prayers and also in literal overseas experiences of ministry.

"God is far more interested in a love relationship with you than He is in what you can do for Him."

—Henry Blackaby,
Experiencing the Word New Testament
(Nashville: Holman Bible Publishers, 2001).

I know of no better way to end this book than with Paul's great hymn of love as found in 1 Corinthians 12:31*b*-13:8*a* (Williams Translation).

"And yet I will show you a way that is better by far: If I could speak the languages of men, of angels too, and have not love, I am only a rattling pan or a clashing cymbal. If I should have the gift of prophecy, and know all secret truths, and knowledge in its every form, and have such perfect faith that I could move mountains, but have no love, I am nothing. If I should dole out everything I have for charity, and give my body up to torture in mere boasting pride, but have no love, I get from it no good at all.

"Love is so patient and so kind; love never boils with jealously; it never boasts, is never puffed with pride; it does not act with rudeness, or insist upon its rights; it never gets provoked, it never harbors evil thoughts; is never glad when wrong is done, but always glad when truth prevails; it bears up under anything, it exercises faith in everything, it keeps up hope in everything, it gives us power to endure in anything. Love never fails."

A Blessing and
a Benediction

I have offered you my hand as we have moved down a number of pathways together. We have been fellow "pilgrims-in-progress," seeking the way to Christ-likeness. Over and over again, we have heard His voice in our times of darkness and confusion, as He has said to us, "Come with Me. Take this path. I will show you the Way."

Now I offer you a blessing—really, God's blessing. May you experience God's abundant resources as you negotiate the twists and turns of each day. May Christ bless you with depths of love and strength below the waterline of your life. May the Holy Spirit fill you to overflowing with the radiant joy and sweetness of Himself. May your life be enriched by this journey so that you will be a beacon, leading others to walk the Father's pathways and to experience His depths.

Very often, I pray for myself and for others a powerful benediction given by the writer of Hebrews. As we part, please allow me to pray these words once again, this time with you in my mind and heart.

"May the God of peace, who through the blood of the eternal covenant brought back from the dead our Lord Jesus, that great Shepherd of the sheep, equip you with everything good for doing his will, and may he work in us what is pleasing to him, through Jesus Christ, to whom be glory for ever and ever. Amen."

—Hebrews 13:20–21

*G*race be with you all.

Suggested Reading

Larry Crabb, *Inside Out* (Colorado Springs: NavPress, 1998).

Richard J. Foster, *Celebration of Discipline: The Path to Spiritual Growth* (San Francisco: Harper San Francisco, 1988).

Richard J. Foster, *Prayer: Finding the Heart's True Home* (San Francisco: Harper San Francisco, 1992).

Trevor Hudson, *Christ-Following: Ten Signposts to Spirituality* (Grand Rapids: Fleming H. Revell, 1996).

Gordon MacDonald, *The Life God Blesses: Weathering the Storms of Life that Threaten the Soul* (Nashville: Thomas Nelson, 1997).

Gordon MacDonald, *Restoring Your Spiritual Passion* (Nashville: Thomas Nelson, 1986).

Henri J. M. Nouwen, *Making All Things New* (San Francisco: Harper San Francisco, 1981).

John Ortberg, *The Life You've Always Wanted* (Grand Rapids: Zondervan, 2002).

John Ortberg, *If You Want to Walk on Water, You've Got to Get Out of the Boat* (Grand Rapids: Zondervan, 2002).

J.I. Packer, *Rediscovering Holiness* (Ann Arbor, MI: Vine Books, 1992).

John Piper, *Desiring God* (Portland, OR: Multnomah Publishers, 2003).

Francis Schaeffer, *True Spirituality* (Wheaton, IL: Tyndale House, 1979).

Gordon T. Smith, *Essential Spirituality* (Nashville: Thomas Nelson, 1994).

Leonard Sweet, *SoulSalsa* (Grand Rapids: Zondervan, 2002).

Gary Thomas, *The Glorious Pursuit: Embracing the Virtues of Christ* (Colorado Springs: NavPress, 1998).

Gary Thomas, *Seeking the Face of God* (Eugene, OR: Harvest House, 1999).

Paul Tournier, *The Meaning of Persons* (New York: Harper & Row, 1957).

Rick Warren, *The Purpose-Driven Life: What on Earth Am I Here For?* (Grand Rapids: Zondervan, 2002).

James Emery White, *You Can Experience…A Spiritual Life* (Nashville: Word, 1999).

Luder G. Whitlock Jr., *The Spiritual Quest: Pursuing Christian Maturity* (Grand Rapids: Baker Book House, 2000).

Donald S. Whitney, *Spiritual Disciplines for the Christian Life* (Colorado Springs: NavPress, 1997).

Dallas Willard, *The Divine Conspiracy: Rediscovering Our Hidden Life in God* (San Francisco: Harper San Francisco, 1998).

Dallas Willard, *Renovation of the Heart: Putting On the Character of Christ* (Colorado Springs: NavPress, 2002).